MW00892252

BBL Books

Bradley Lewis

Mickey Cohen: The Rat Pack Years
The Elder Statesman's Life and Times
1960-1976

Also by Bradley Lewis

Dissolution
Cul De Sac
Another Bad Day In Beverly Hills
Mickey Cohen and the West Coast Mob
   Washington's Crackdown on Vegas and Los Angeles
   1950-1960
God's Helix
Great White Doctor
Hollywood's Celebrity Gangster, The
   Incredible Life and Times of Mickey Cohen
The Bloomingdale Code
My Father, Uncle Miltie
Mickey Cohen: The Gangster Squad and the Mob
   The True Story of Vice in Los Angeles 1937-1950

www.bradleylewis.org

First edition
Abridged Version of Hollywood's Celebrity Gangster

Printed in the United States of America

Library of Congress Cataloging-in-Publication Data

Lewis, Bradley.

1. Cohen, Mickey, 1914–1976. 2. Criminals--California--
Los Angeles--Biography. 3. Gangsters--California--Los
Angeles--Biography. 4. Jewish criminals--United States--
Biography. 5. Organized crime--California--Los Angeles--
History.

HV6248.C64 L49 2007
364.109/2

For MR

The criminal has no hates or fears—
except very personal ones. He is possibly
the only human left in the world who
looks lovingly on society.

—Ben Hecht
Screenwriter and author

1.

$_D$espite all his cumulative troubles and his dreadful relationship with the Kennedys, Mickey still played his role as an honorary member of the developing Rat Pack. Whether it was social or politics, his efforts never ceased, not even while he waited for his pending new tax trial.

During his tenure, all of his well-known contacts may have helped his business and publicity, but in later years, those same associations led many to place him at the core of the worst-case conspiracy theories, a voyeuristic peek between the sheets of celebrities and politicians.[1]

Insinuations and direct accusations exist regarding Mickey's specific connections to both Kennedy assassinations, the suspicious death of Marilyn Monroe, and the extensive efforts to cover up the horrific events.

Like Woody Allen's Zelig, Mickey pops up in a series of unlikely historic episodes, alternatively disguised as a Machiavellian politician, two-faced lover, or confidant. Beyond accusers' sometimes-amusing agenda-motivated claims, including anti-Semitic overtones, are theories based on his unusual liaisons, connecting him to nefarious national and international activities.

Theorists blame Mickey and Meyer Lansky, because of their extensive Israeli interests, for a variety of American tragedies. National Jewish organizations were continually fundraising for Israel, and the Jewish mob was no exception, protecting the larger community from anti-Semites, as they had done locally for generations. Charitable and political connections to Israel provided the Jewish syndicate recognition, legitimacy, and the approval of their established mainstream brethren.

Fundraising was the proper entry to upscale synagogues, country clubs, and Jewish-sponsored events.

Mickey certainly enjoyed hobnobbing with the Jewish elite, but he instinctively wanted to protect the Jewish state. Israel remained the central political issue for him during the 1960 presidential election.

Clearly, Menachem Begin, an Israeli acquaintance of his, or any politician, was not befriending Mickey for Las Vegas comps or the female companionship he supplied. However, it would have benefited Begin or any Israeli operative to have inside information about John Kennedy. Was JFK a friend to Israel? Could the Jews count on Kennedy? If elected, the fate of Israel would be in his hands, and Mickey knew that as well as anyone.[1]

He had abstained from helping JFK: "Frank [Sinatra] didn't particularly ask me to do anything for the Kennedy campaign." Not that Mickey avidly volunteered, or the Kennedys wanted anything to do with him. Despite his friendship with Nixon, Mickey did acknowledge that he thought Kennedy was the best of the bunch seeking the presidency.

Nixon's defeat by Kennedy in 1960 was no help to Mickey's cause. Not only was the fate of Israeli support unknown, but his own Washington connections were dramatically diminished—the Kennedys would never help him, particularly with his tax dilemma. Author John Davis referred to him as one of the Kennedys' "most determined enemies."[2]

Mickey said that the Democrats stole the election in Chicago, and Republicans had ample reason to believe him. Mobster Sam Giancana would boast about how he put JFK in the White House. Mickey confessed the mob's political realities: "I know that certain people in the Chicago organization knew that they had to get

4

John Kennedy in. There was no thought that they were going to get the best of it with John Kennedy. See, there may be different guys running for an office, and none of them may be the solution to what's best for a combination..."

The Giancanas in writing their book were privy to some of the details:

To assure the election's outcome, guys either trucked people from precinct to precinct and poll to poll so they could vote numerous times or stood menacingly alongside voting booths, where they made it clear to prospective voters that all ballots were to be cast for Kennedy.

Mobsters like Giancana and Rosselli expected special treatment in return. Mickey knew that Sinatra spoke to all the Kennedys, including Joe, requesting a soft touch from the new regime. Robert Kennedy left Sinatra cold, and Giancana lost confidence in Sinatra's Kennedy connection.

Many also reported cheating by the Republicans, but obviously not at the skill level of the Democrats, whose own mob machine out-foxed Nixon's mobsters.

While Mickey had a polarized association with the Kennedys, he had a perverse one with Marilyn Monroe, whom he does not mention in his memoir. Former investigator Gary Wean had observed Mickey's handsome boys Sam LoCigno and Georgie Piscitelle, escorting Marilyn all over town, including Barney Ruditsky's Plymouth House and a motel on Van Nuys Boulevard in the Valley. On one occasion Wean heard a bedroom recording of Marilyn, part of Mickey's extortion racquets. Mickey had tapes of her having sex with both Georgie and Sam. He thought that his attractive professional pimp Piscitelle could persuade her to talk about her dalliances with JFK. He believed that he could leverage Kennedy once he started having sex with Marilyn. Blackmail was no stranger to Mickey; it was part of the business.

The hazy source for the above material is a party girl named Mary Mercadante, who also worked for Georgie, and became eager to turn against Mickey since Georgie found Marilyn more attractive. According to Wean, Mercadante also told him, "Cohen got mad and told Georgie to stick with Marilyn and pour drinks or pills down her, whatever it takes and find out what John Kennedy intended to do about financing Israel."

Mickey definitely wanted a closer connection to JFK, and it was through Monroe that he got that link. He was the king when it came to manipulation. While some credit Sinatra with making the Monroe connection to the White House—Sinatra introduced Marilyn to JFK at Peter Lawford's Malibu beach house, a popular show biz hangout—there is evidence that it was really Mickey. The Lawford compound was renamed "High Anus Port," likely by Rat Pack wordsmith Sammy Cahn. Everyone but Kennedy sister Pat Lawford seemed aware that the locale was the "in" place for wild sex. Commented Marilyn Monroe, who had taken to hair dye jobs below the waist, "Poor Pat's so out of touch... She probably thinks we're playing football" (the popular Kennedy pastime).

The shared credit goes to Mickey pal comedian and Rat Pack regular Joey Bishop for making the *shidech*—Yiddish for "match." According to Wean, Bishop was personally responsible for setting up JFK with Marilyn during the presidential campaign in 1960. "It was Joey Bishop that came up with the idea of a wild party for JFK. He talked Lawford into it." Wean persists based on ethnic bonds: "Bishop was a Jew and real tight

8

with Cohen"; and further makes his case: "Bishop knew Kennedy would be taken by the Monroe sex appeal."

When it came to women, Mickey and the Rat Pack passed them around like dispensable commodities. The mob and show business crowds mingled in a very small community, where any attractive starlet-in-training would be introduced around as part of an unspoken courtesy. Mickey, JFK, and Sinatra dated some of the same women. On occasion, Mickey told Sinatra to stop sending the shared women to Washington—some brought to the White House under cover of night. Mickey claimed that JFK needed two to three women per day. Marilyn would confide the details to Sinatra's assistant George Jacobs, outlining JFK's obsession with sex. The locations included fancy suites at the Plaza in New York, as well as broom closets at the Vegas Sands. "That guy [JFK] would say *anything* to score!"

Gossipy Monroe blabbed that he suffered from premature ejaculation, something she preferred to attribute to her irresistible charms, and his preoccupation with the presidency. She preferred Sinatra in bed. "He's the best... And *I* should know." Sinatra would never forgive the boys for arranging a Monroe tryst with Robert Kennedy.[3] It was likely during RFK's Hollywood romp with screenwriter Budd Schulberg and movie macher Jerry Wald for production of the younger Kennedy's anticrime book, *The Enemy Within*. Former Monroe husband Joe DiMaggio did his best to bar the entire Rat Pack from Marilyn's funeral.

"Frank [Sinatra] got him [JFK] all the broads he could ever have used... I guess they preferred to go to bed with John Kennedy instead of Mickey Cohen, you know—Frank Sinatra instead of Mickey Cohen," Mickey surmised in later years.

Not all the political ladies declined Mickey's company, and he made of point of emphasizing the quality of his philandering: "And these girls were not unknowns. They were all starlets."

The Kennedy list featured Judith Exner Campbell,[4] Angie Dickinson, Jayne Mansfield, Kim Novak, and the aforementioned Marilyn Monroe. Lesser famous names included Mary Meyer,[5] and the unknown blondes from the White House secretarial pool whom JFK codenamed "Fiddle and Faddle." Jackie Kennedy preferred the term "White House dogs." The White House was not off limits for JFK's guests.

Many linked Exner to Mickey, particularly since she was close to clothier and Mickey associate Sy Devore, who dressed the Rat Pack, and had run Slapsy Maxie's.

Exner, who first met Dean Martin at age seventeen, would eventually work her way up to JFK after an introduction by Sinatra, but not before a dalliance with papa Joe Kennedy, who loved his stays at the Sinatra-Lawford-Giancana Lake Tahoe Cal-Neva Lodge and Casino. When visiting Sinatra in Palm Springs, Joe Kennedy insisted that Sinatra cover his expenses for his "date" with the then Judy Campbell. She once told a press conference that she gave up sex with Sinatra because he was too kinky. Sinatra's public answer: "Hell hath no fury like a hustler with a literary agent."

Sinatra maintained an apartment, complete with private pool, at the Sands Hotel in Vegas. At this poolside lair, Exner had her first of many dinners with JFK, with whom she would carry on an affair until 1962. Sinatra also introduced her to Sam Giancana in Florida. She dated Kennedy and martini-drinker Giancana at the same time and in her book mentions that Kennedy was fond of the occasional ménage a trois. Both he and

Giancana spoke on the telephone with Exner's impressionable mother, who was pleased that her daughter was dating such important men.[6]

Thin-built Robert Blakely, former chief counsel and staff director of the House Select Committee on Assassinations, links Exner's promiscuity to JFK's demise: "From the mob's point of view, Kennedy had been compromised. He had crossed the line. In the Greek sense, the liaison with Judith Campbell was, we came to believe, Kennedy's fatal flaw, the error in judgment for which the gods would demand their due." The mob viewed Kennedy as vulnerable, perhaps too much like them.

For the Exner introduction and likely many other reasons, Jackie Kennedy couldn't stomach Sinatra.[7] She was happy when he fell out of favor with the entire Kennedy circle, and they refused to stay at his Palm Springs residence, opting instead for

Bing Crosby's house. This followed a visit from FBI Director Hoover to President Kennedy identifying the Exner-Giancana connection. Peter Lawford, Rat Packer and husband of Kennedy's sister Pat, who himself had been initially rejected by patriarch Joseph P. Kennedy, would take the blame. Longtime friend Sam Giancana would hold Sinatra accountable for his own political downfall.[8]

After JFK's election, there were always problems with Sinatra's Rat Pack associations. Columnists Dorothy Kilgallen and Ruth Montgomery, who worked for Hearst, needled the White House about its relationship with the fabled entertainers who had ties to Mickey and other nationally connected mobsters. Kilgallen wrote during the election: "The situation was becoming especially delicate in Massachusetts, where important church figures don't quite understand the Sinatra-Kennedy connection."

Writer Joe Hyams, Mickey's friend and a Hollywood mainstay, published articles that were also critical of the Rat Pack for their seedy associations. Sinatra tried to push the accusations aside: "The various guilds that are part of my professional life are the only organized groups to which I belong."

Peter Lawford did his share of public spin:

> Now look—that Clan business—I mean that's hokey. I mean it makes us sound like children—like we all wore sweat shirts that said "The Clan" and Frank with a whistle around his neck. They make us sound so unsavory. We're just a lot of people on the same wavelength. We like each other. What's wrong with that?

Comedian Joey Bishop milked the subject with "Clan, Clan, Clan. I'm sick and tired of hearing things about the

Clan—just because a few of us guys get together once a week with sheets over our heads!"

When Sinatra and hard-drinking cocaine user Lawford first opened Puccini, at fancy 224 South Beverly Drive, Mickey was one of its famous regular customers. He remained a recalcitrant Sinatra friend, something that Lawford despised. Lawford did not like Sinatra's mob associations. When Puccini first opened, "Mr. Television" Milton Berle quipped, "If Kennedy is elected, will Puccini's be the summer White House?" (Puccini had four other partners whose names never appeared in the papers.)

On February 12, 1961, at twelve-fifteen in the morning, an angry Mickey stormed inside Puccini and headed for comedian Red Skelton's manager, who was dining with actor George Raft.

The eight customers and the bartender froze to watch him zoom in on his target. Like a well-scripted B-movie, two goons took their places inside the front door to stand guard. Red's manager was having an affair with Red's wife—or so Mickey thought. He actually jumped up on the booth's table and started kicking Red's manager.

Raft tried to intercede but Mickey was firm. "You shut up, Raft, or you know what you're gonna get."

Mickey slapped the manager around yelling, "This is for you, you no good S.O.B." He put him in the hospital.

Outside the restaurant, the Lilliputian fighter and his *shtarkers* met a third party, who upon hearing what had happened walked inside and informed Red's ailing manager, "You should consider yourself lucky, you're supposed to be dead now."

Red's manager denied to Beverly Hills police that any physical attack took place. He also insisted that he was dining alone that night, but did say that Mickey had given him some sound advice concerning Red Skelton.

The story mushroomed through the media. The police regularly sent eager undercover cops to feast at chichi Puccini. The restaurant now had a national reputation as a Mafia hangout for Sinatra's friends. When business slacked off Lawford blamed Mickey, and overlooked the larger picture of Sinatra's need to associate with unsavory characters.

On May 4, 1961, forty-nine-year-old Max Tannenbaum was the victim of a hit outside a bar owned by Max Lerner. Mickey's crony Tannenbaum survived, nearly lost an eye, and faced misdemeanor charges for having burglar's tools in his car.

Despite all the publicity over the discovery of organized crime in America, on May 5, 1961, the FBI closed all its extensive Anti-Racketeering files on Mickey. It appeared that the IRS had nailed him again, and the FBI felt confident in the case.

2.

Like celebrities in trouble multiple times today, Mickey could not bring himself to accept that he could be prosecuted a second time for the same crime.

The indictment had moved ahead efficiently. He faced a maximum sentence of thirty-two years and a $65,000 fine. If the judge and jury imposed the worst-case scenario, his life would be over. The *New York Times* noted that he was forty-seven.

When it was time to face the music, unlike today, there were no trial experts to coach Mickey. He always walked into court with the same story. His plan was to convince the judge and jury of the silly notion that appeared in the papers; he lived on loans. He must have sounded like a child caught in a lie, while thoroughly prepared prosecutors listened to the fable. What could his attorneys have been thinking? Did his defense team roll over after pressure from federal authorities and high-ranking politicians? His attorneys had many prior opportunities to prepare him with better records and functioning shell companies that shifted untraceable cash. Tax attorneys had already done the same for much of the syndicate, but not for Mickey, who left himself vulnerable.

At the request of lead IRS agent Donald F. Bowler, seventeen tax districts had reported to the IRS to help nail Mickey on the new tax evasion rap. The under $400,000 sum appeared paltry compared to the huge amounts of cash generated by his and other mobsters' action.

The *Los Angeles Times* described Mickey as five foot three, with thin black hair and elevator shoes. He audaciously showed up

at his trial with lists of people who had
lent him money, including his own
mother, Fanny Cohen (Fanny Friedman—
she was married to Charles Friedman),
Sarah Cohen (Mrs. Sammy Cohen, his
brother Sammy's widow), and comedian
Jimmy Durante, who purportedly paid part
of Mickey's fines the first time around. He
behaved as if his life was going to continue
without interruption.

The trial covered everything the agents
could dig up. Not all parties invited by the
well-armed prosecutors were located, and
several said that they had never heard of
Mickey. The prosecution called a
monstrous 194 witnesses. The process
generated 8,000 pages of reporter's
transcript, 947 government exhibits, and
27 defense exhibits. The witness list at the
trial read like a who's who of Hollywood.
Ben Hecht, Jerry Lewis, Red Skelton, and
welterweight Don Jordan all testified.
Stripper Candy Barr and "dancer" Beverly
Hills added the surreal air that had become

22

part of all Hollywood-related trials.
(Mickey felt that Hills' testimony didn't
help his case.)

Mickey's own nephew Allan Weiner
testified regarding almost $23,000 in
checks that he had issued or endorsed for
him. Weiner said that he didn't remember
any of the checks, although the signatures
looked like his. He maintained that his
handwriting was evolving, related to year-
long psychiatric meetings. He had worked
for Mickey attorney Paul Caruso, at
Mickey's flower shop, and the Carousel
ice-cream parlor that Mickey's mother
officially owned. He didn't remember
storing fifty grand in his personal account
by age nineteen, with some of the money
originally earmarked for his uncle.

U.S. Attorney Sheridan grilled Mickey's
gray-haired sister Lillian Weiner. She had
been the owner and president of Michael's
Greenhouse, but had no recollection of
$30,000 in cash deposits made to the
business during Mickey's tenure as its

super salesman. She acknowledged that
monthly deposits usually ran between
$300 and $7,000, with only one $800
amount paid regularly by a chain of restaurants. Mickey's sister remained firm, and
said that she did not recall the reason for
several deposits in the thousands. She was
also unable to recognize any signatures,
with one exception, "that one could be my
signature." Her credo became, "I don't
remember right now."

Estranged attorney Paul Caruso took the
stand and discussed his fee dispute with
Mickey. He said that Mickey told him,
"Don't worry about it—you'll get paid."
Caruso said that he was still out $7,900.

Mickey's attorney Jack Dahlstrum
approached the bench, and after a three-
minute conference, Judge Boldt dismissed
Caruso, but said that he should make
himself available for furthering
questioning.

Aubrey V. Stemler, the vending machine
manufacturer, agreed that he had given

Mickey loans totaling $15,000 in exchange for a healthy ten percent of Mickey's life story. Stemler's contract called for a repayment of the money at six percent if no motion picture materialized.

Joseph E. Bishop, manager to Ben Blue and the entertainer's Santa Monica club, only received two percent of the movie venture for $7,500.

Despite Mickey's hapless first meeting with Jackie Gleason, the unlikely and chubby duo developed a decent relationship down the road. Former fight promoter Barney Peller testified that he had loaned Mickey $1,000 since Mickey promised Gleason the lead in a movie called *Gus the Great*. Peller had owned the rights to a novel that was the basis for the screenplay. At the trial, he said that Gleason had agreed to do the movie, but later backed out when he lost the rights. He also paid bills for Mickey when he stayed at the Terrace Hilton in Cincinnati, and on one occasion sent him $1,500 in money orders.

Publisher and evangelist W. C. Jones had sent attorney Rexford Eagan, who worked with Jerry Geisler, a $1,000 check to pay for Mickey's legal fees. Jones also testified that he had forked over $5,000 to Mickey during his alleged conversion to Christianity.

As mentioned earlier, the Krause family had given Mickey $25,000 for an interest in his book and movie. With a straight face, Dr. Krause told the prosecutor that he had expected Mickey to commit himself for psychiatric study in return for the loan. His interest in Mickey's theatrical venture was worth a huge ten percent, according to the contract. His sister had sent Mickey an additional $10,000, through Chicago mob lawyer George Bieber. The psychiatrist had halfheartedly asked Mickey to refund his money.

Dr. Krause told the crowded courtroom, "...greatly interested in Mr. Cohen when I first met him...gentle nice man." He told the jury that his own movie aspirations were minimal and that he was more interested in Mickey's "past history, present behavior, present symptomology, the way he behaves and what motivates his behavior."

More of the doctor's own personality profile materialized when oil lease dealer Nate Suess took the stand and said that Krause was a "big speculator." The Hollywood Boulevard oilman had introduced Krause to Mickey.

Theatrical agent Lou Irwin had given Mickey a grand to invest in the movie on his life. Irwin took the Hollywood high road; a thousand bucks was nothing to hand out: he always handed out cash at the end of the week for actors to survive the weekend.

Phil Packer, the greeter at Rondelli's, home of the Whalen shooting, had loaned

Mickey $9,500. Mickey had given him a diamond watch and fancy ring for security.

When asked about his association with bank president Harold Brown, Mickey answered, "I helped him make money and so naturally he thought kindly of me."

One of Mickey's interior decorators, William K. Howard, tried to come to his defense even though Mickey still owed him about $8,000. Howard had designed a stainless steel kitchen, remote controlled draperies, stocked the dining area cabinets with china and silver service, and installed a typewriter and adding machine in the business section of the apartment.

He overstated his case when he said that Mickey "always paid the tabs wherever he went." He made a huge mistake when he said that Mickey sometimes carried thirty grand in cash. He, and many others who testified, were either ignorant of, or didn't care about, the tax laws. Howard, upon further questioning and perhaps a few dirty looks from the defense team, recanted and said that he hadn't really seen the money, perhaps only a $100 bill.

The IRS contributed many unreported Mickey money exchanges as evidence. The twenty-three grand front money for Michael's Greenhouse had come from colorful attorney George Bieber. After prison, Mickey had received welcome home money from Thomas Vaughn, a New Orleans businessman. Babe McCoy, a famous boxing impresario, who occasionally suffered from his friendship with Mickey—Chief Parker was convinced that McCoy fixed fights—had also chipped in $6,000. Restaurateur Morris Orloff, who once won a suit against the Los Angeles Turf Club for denying him entry based on his unsavory reputation, gladly added his ten grand to the "restore Mickey foundation."

Mickey could not provide any evidence of a consistent form of legitimate income, and didn't try. He was a victim of his own sloppy accounting, dinosaur record keeping, and blinding stubbornness.

The convoluted messy list of non-reported income had one fairy tale ending. Mickey had taken over two grand from Cincinnati tree surgeon Charles Schneider; Barney Peller had introduced the two men in Cincinnati. Schneider wanted his twelve-year-old daughter Janet to get into show business—who better to ask than impresario Mickey? Mickey first introduced her to Red Skelton and Frank Sinatra. The Schneiders met everyone, from Danny Thomas to Bobby Darin, and Edward G. Robinson to Don Rickles. Janet appeared on television with Louis Armstrong and Jerry Lewis. Schneider also gave Mickey another $2,500 for his life story. He told authorities that he had no complaints about Mickey.

Jerry Lewis, on Wednesday, May 24, told the packed courtroom how he had loaned Mickey $5,000 in cash without any security or written contract "because he needed help." He also spoke about how he had helped further the career of young Janet Schneider, arranged a guest appearance for her on his television show, but despite her talent could not hire her for the entire 1957–1958 season because of skittish sponsors who preferred big name acts.

Jerry explained seriously how he had entered into discussions as a movie producer for Mickey's life story, citing Robert Mitchum as a better casting choice. He said that any production utilizing his skill "should deal with levity—for some strange reason that's what people expect. It would be difficult for me to apply myself to this [the Mickey Cohen story] concept."

When Jerry was ready to leave the courtroom Red Skelton took his turn in the hot-seat-turned-P.R. chair.

He taunted Red. "Let's see how funny you are going to be. Let's see you get a laugh."

Red did. The standing room only crowd got its "money's worth."

Skelton typified Hollywood's cynical wink-wink attitude toward the mob. He had met Mickey in early 1957 at Los Angeles International Airport when they were seeing off mutual friends. Mickey kept up the relationship, often sending greeting cards and gifts for the Skelton children.

Mickey was a close enough friend to ask Skelton for five grand at a time—his regular quick-cash routine at dinner. Red always paid.

When Assistant U.S. Attorney Thomas Sheridan asked Red if he had any financial dealings with Mickey, Red replied, "None whatsoever—except paying for this trial, as a taxpayer, I mean."

He pressed Red and asked, "You pay your taxes do you, Mr. Skelton?"

Red did not feel he had to succumb to the prosecutor's style. "You know I do. I'm allergic to that bay up there."

He explained that Mickey was welcome at rehearsals for his television show and often brought friends. He could not remember much about singer Janet.

"She couldn't have sung because of the facilities in our house. We have a Hammond organ and nobody can play the thing," Red told the judge.

Judge Boldt jumped into the act. "Can't you play it yourself?"

"Yes," answered Red, his head bowed. "But just by the numbers on the book."

The judge jumped at the opportunity to illustrate his show business acumen and said, "You're not a bad straight man."

Red discussed the $15,000 that Billy Graham had promised Mickey to attend the revival meeting in Madison Square Garden. He also said that Graham had promised Mickey an additional $25,000 if he converted to Christianity.

During his eclectic casting call, Mickey had also asked the lean six-foot comedian to consider the lead in his movie. Red had politely declined the role, and Mickey later confessed to him that he was just fishing for a star name: "Well, it was just a shot in the dark."

When asked by the prosecutor about appearing in Mickey's movie, Red stated the obvious. "I couldn't see myself—or I should say, Mickey—as a tall redheaded fellow." It drew big laughs.

During the hearing, Mickey brazenly admitted that he had run a gambling operation in the Ambassador Hotel during the late forties with the imprimatur of hotel operators Myer and David Schine, of Schine Enterprises. Perhaps he thought that the admission might distract his prosecutors, and he would end up pleading to a lesser crime.

He bragged to his interrogators about the high-roller entourage that floated in and out of the luxurious hotel. "...I've seen $30,000 to $50,000 exchange hands in one roll." (The *Los Angeles Times* ran a quote from the hotel management on June

21, 1961: "Mickey Cohen did not operate
any gambling concerns in this hotel to our
knowledge. If he did, he did it
surreptitiously.")

Mickey also owned seven gaming
operations throughout the United States
and three within Los Angeles. Each one
brought in over $80,000 per month. The
big casinos were at Dincara, San
Bernardino, Lake Arrowhead, and Watts.

Judge Boldt had made sure that the
jurors, seven men and five women, had the
thirty-nine page index to all the material
introduced at the eight-week trial. The
federal judge lectured the jury for nearly
three hours. The agents had compiled a
strong case against Mickey by overloading
the evidence on an already tainted dossier.

The jury heard final arguments on June
27. The forty days in court ended on June
30. Reporters speculated that Mickey
might get forty years, one for each day of
the trial. The jury took only twenty-two
and one-half hours to put Mickey away;

they convicted him on eight counts, while acquitting him on five others. The inevitable had become a reality, and attorney Bieber could not save him.

Before sentencing, Judge Boldt made his position clear regarding Mickey's obvious business style: "...he has followed a fantastically extravagant way of living without paying any income tax...without productive employment or visible means of self-support..." The sometimes-affable judge sentenced Mickey to fifteen years and $30,000 in fines on Monday, July 1, 1961.

Mickey clasped his hands and bowed his head when he heard the verdict.

He took time later outside the courtroom to make his feelings known. "They convicted me because I am Mickey Cohen. They thought they had to." He may not have realized how close the statement was to the truth.

Mickey was the victim of multiple vendettas. In addition to his criminal activities, his punishment was as much for being a long-term pain in the ass and consistent wise guy to his enemies. His public notoriety had come back to haunt him. Because of his celebrity, authorities insisted on the most severe approach.

Mechanisms existed for early release, with some based on good behavior and many mobsters bought early parole through political channels. Authorities offered Mickey an opportunity to escape any incarceration by ratting on Paul Ricca and Tony Accardo. He declined, and remained a *stand-up guy.*

To add insult to the injury of a repeat trial, the Los Angeles police confiscated his remaining custom-built Cadillac.

Mickey said goodbye to his regular routine: the Beverly Hills Health Club, Gaiety Deli, Largo Night Club, Cloisters, Crescendo, Carousel Ice Cream Parlor, Coconut Grove, La Rue, Top's On The Strip, the Moulin Rouge, and Slate Brothers.

On July 28, he flew in a Border Patrol plane to take him back to the hellhole Alcatraz. When he began his fifteen-year sentence, the prison population consisted of only sixty-four inmates; it could house between 260 and 275. The dismal structure was in disrepair; not that it was ever the darling of the penal system.

"It was a crumbling dungeon. At the time I was in Alcatraz it was only for personal enemies of Bobby Kennedy," he said retrospectively.

RFK, appointed attorney general in 1961, announced that Mickey would continue to be a priority target, and initiated a new full investigation. It was as much a vendetta for the hot exchanges during the McClellan hearings as it was a need to clean up organized crime.[1]

Mickey was taken by surprise.

But nobody in my line of work had an idea that he [JFK] was going to name Bobby Kennedy attorney general. That was the last thing anyone thought. In fact, he had just openly promised in his campaign that he wouldn't name Bobby as attorney general.

From the mob's perspective, this was hardly a small double-cross.

While he was in prison, microphone surveillance continued in many of his businesses and associations, including the Dunes Hotel in Vegas. Robert Kennedy had started the new wiretaps and eavesdropping, and the system would continue through 1965 and beyond, under Attorney General Katzenbach.

The convoluted legal process made appeals difficult. After much legal wrangling, authorities begrudgingly released Mickey on October 17, 1961, having served eighty-two days of his long sentence.[2]

The *New York Times* mentioned that Mickey, now reported to be fifty years old, was unhappy because his now twenty-year-old blonde girlfriend Sandy Hagen did not meet him when authorities released him on bail.

He told reporters when he got off the prison launch at Fort Mason, "I expect to marry her as soon as I get permission... It depends on the advice of my attorneys and what the law permits."

The national attention to his plight forced FBI boss Hoover to answer letters from the public. Some constituents complained about Mickey's release.

Mickey lived up to the naysayers. He beat up a Teamsters Union picket, and stole his sign. The negative publicity complicated the ongoing appeals process for his attorneys.

Mickey was out on bail only two weeks when police arrested him. A grand jury had geared up to reopen the murder case of Jack "The Enforcer" Whalen, with new information about the missing murder weapon. Superior Judge Evelle J. Younger initially denied bail for Mickey. Multiple attorneys appealed the decision, including A. L. Wirin, Paul Augustine, Jr., Ward Sullivan, and Al Mathews.

Mickey told reporters, "What can I say? It's a complete roust."

The new Whalen indictment followed three days of closed-door sessions, pushed forward by persistent Deputy District Attorneys James Ford and Joseph Busch. Mickey voluntarily arrived for his booking with attorney Wirin, and bail bondsman Abe Phillips, the usual arrest entourage. Phillips always brought an old set of clothes for Mickey, since he dressed to the nines for the photographers, and then changed before entering his cell. He was soon out on bail.

Police also arrested handsome Georgie Piscitelle, now thirty, at his home on 8214 Sunset Boulevard, and listed his occupation as a liquor salesman. They arrested Joe DiCarlo, no longer Candy Barr's manager, at a café in Santa Monica.

Movie producer Roger Leonard was arrested as he arrived at University of Pennsylvania Hospital to visit his wife who had gall bladder problems. Leonard told police that he was working on filming scenes for his brother Herbert, the producer of the immensely popular television series *Route 66.*

David Marcus and Paul Augustine stood by their client Lo Cigno's earlier trial and issued a statement, "two years ago this was a classic self-defense case involving only LoCigno and Whalen and it still is."

At an appeal to reduce his prison sentence for tax evasion, Mickey played a television interview in which he appeared contrite, and appeared confident that he might get off.

At holiday time 1961, he was the focus of a feature story by Ron Rieder of the *Valley News.* Forty-eight-year-old Mickey included his twenty-year-old girlfriend Sandy Hagen in the piece told to Rieder, with both subjects benefiting differently from Mickey's revisionist aging. He lived in a rented house in Van Nuys, a less expensive neighborhood in the San Fernando Valley.[3]

"As long as he is quiet and doesn't cause any trouble around here, he is as good as any other neighbor," said a local.

"It's better than a bunch of drunks and rowdies," added another citizen.

From his lawn chair near the swimming pool, Mickey was soft-spoken and candid about his life. He wore a white sweater with his initials monogrammed over his heart. The doormat also had the initials "M C" carved in the center. Under the sunny California sun, Mickey reveled in telling the details of his home expenses, only two hundred a month, and "They even pay for gas and electric and a gardener takes care of the place." He complained about the lack of closet space; his clothes lacked organization, more were still in boxes. The hot water tank, of course, was not big enough to accommodate his unusual shower usage.

Rieder noted that aside from Mickey's pending tax appeal, he would go to trial on March 5 for the reopened Whalen case. A District Court of Appeal had set aside the original murder conviction in the murder, allowing the judge to order a second trial for LoCigno.

Mickey rehearsed the Whalen details again. "I've been shot at so many times, when I heard those shots, I just ducked. It was pretty dark in there anyway. I didn't even see the gun fired."

He and Sandy displayed the rings they had exchanged with her parents' blessing. The government forbade a marriage until the outcome of the tax case.

Another article in the *Nation* mentioned that Mickey's silk pajamas now cost $275.

Writer Joe Hyams, who also lived in the Valley, had replaced Hecht as the author of Mickey's life story. Mickey continued to shop the movie rights to any suckers who were impressed by the newspaper articles outlining his venture. The working title for Hyams' book was the unfortunate *The Poison Has Left Me.*

On January 12, 1962, the United States Court of Appeals affirmed Mickey's conviction and declined bail. U.S. Supreme Court Justice Douglas agreed with Mickey's interpretation; the IRS had convicted him twice for the same offense.

Sandy-the-girlfriend saw Mickey off as he again prepared for prison. He wore a cream-colored jacket and light slacks, brown and white shoes, and Hollywood sunglasses for the prison cruise.

Sandy lamented, "I'll wait for Mickey...and I'm going to try and lead a normal life despite the publicity."

After what appeared to be one last holiday season on the outside, Mickey headed back to Alcatraz on January 12. When he boarded the heavily guarded launch that would take him across the bay, he paused on the gangplank for photographs with his hands already cuffed.

On January 30, Justice Douglas issued a second release order, pending Supreme Court action and $100,000 bail. On February 17, Mickey was free on bail again.[4]

The second Whalen trial began. An actress named Ann Root testified against all the diners at the Italian dinner at Rondelli's. A USC psychology student with a penchant for dating people in the fast lane, she had hung around with Mickey and Joe DiCarlo.

Joey Bishop was dragged into the mix by DiCarlo's lawyer Harvey Byron, and somewhat came to Mickey's and DiCarlo's rescue. Author Shawn Levy spotted the irony in the moment. "All the creeps that Frank liked to run with, all the thugs whom Dean and Sammy worked for, all the awful shit Peter was in on—guess who was the only one ever to testify at a murder trial: Joey."

Bishop told the new jury that stripper Candy Barr's theatrical agent and four-year friend Joseph DiCarlo had invited him to dinner, but true to form, Bishop had cancelled. His own character assassination was his best defense for removing himself from the scene of the crime: "I have a reputation for not keeping dinner engagements. So, how could I have been there?"

Bishop spoke of his lengthy golf day; he claimed that he had played forty-five holes. He was too tired to drive to Rondelli's, but not tired enough to stay home. Bishop had invited DiCarlo to catch his act at the Cloister Club on the Strip later that evening.

Mickey's defense was simple: "It was the hottest place in town. So when the move was made to knock Whalen in, would I blow up my own joint?"

DiCarlo's was similar—why would he have invited Joey Bishop to dinner at Rondelli's the night of a planned hit?

The jury of eleven women and one man was deadlocked nine to three on April 10 after five days of deliberation. Superior Court Judge Lewis Drucker declared a mistrial without clarifying the disposition of the nine jurors.

Mickey waited for the final appeals process to run its course, and was back in custody on May 8, 1962. His attorneys had exhausted all avenues of appeal.

No dice.

Mickey told reporters when he surrendered on a Tuesday, "I don't feel too good about it."

Sandy Hagen stood by and cried in her handkerchief.

Mickey offered up his philosophy: "If the Supreme Court thinks this is the kind of sentence I should have, that's the way it's going to be."

Over two hundred people watched him as he held his own court outside the Civic Center Federal Building in Los Angeles. He wore a tan silk suit with a gold monogram on the pocket and dabbed cologne behind his ears as he spoke.

Attorney A. L. Wirin and bondsman Abe Phillips stood by him as he told reporters how he had visited his aged mother the night before.

Autograph seekers blocked Mickey's entry to the courtroom. He obliged his fans until Wirin called him away.

When the formalities ended, he made a final statement: "I always been decent and right."

He then kissed Sandy and said, "I followed the concept of life man should—except for that gambling operation."

Later, when it was time to leave the courtroom, Mickey picked up two brown paper bags that held his clean underwear and socks. The unflattering AP wire described the two towering marshals who sandwiched the "short, balding, plump little man" as he left for prison.

He returned to Alcatraz to resume his original sentence on May 14, 1962. His full term release date was December 13, 1976. His first parole eligibility date would be December 1966. The understanding of the FBI was that his Mandatory Release date was January 1972.

The changing political climate had influenced Mickey's harsh sentencing, had hurt his chances of successful appeal, and would likewise complicate early parole.

Ironically, 1962 was the year J. Edgar Hoover came out of the closet, not about his rumored sexual preferences, but about recognizing organized crime. The FBI announced the astonishing turnaround, including the discovery of a ten-million-dollar white slave trade (a popular government and FBI term for prostitution) that catered to mob-controlled casinos and nightclubs.

The FBI bragged publicly that it had recovered over 17,000 stolen cars the previous year, an all-time record. The stagnant organization still clung to past victories, operated as a federal fat cat, and was afraid to risk its reputation by tackling the highest level of organized crime. While it appeared to have altered its political agenda with regard to Mickey's syndicate life, his prison life became the target of an unexpected full-scale intensive investigation.

By September 1962 the FBI employed 6,000 federal agents, and had the available work force and inclination to make Mickey's prison life a hardship. Alcatraz was already one of the worst examples of the penal system in the United States.

3.

$_M$ickey and Al Capone were the only tax evaders ever sent to Alcatraz. Some said that it was cruel and unusual punishment for Mickey. Alcatraz was no Club Fed; the grim decrepit Rock was the worst example of malignant neglect.

Mickey was unable to come to terms with his fate and the substandard prison conditions that he thought he could improve. According to him, there were no playing cards, magazines, newspapers, televisions, or radios. The library was antiquated and filled with crumbling, yellowed pages. He was unable to get any candy, except perhaps during holidays.

He maintained his own protective clique: some very well-known criminals like Frankie Carbo, Freddie Stein, likeable Harlem boss Bumpy Johnson, and public enemy number one Alvin Karpis, who had worked the Barker-Karpis gang. Between all of their contacts, there must have been an occasional piece of candy to share.[1]

Mickey did confess that San Francisco's Paoli's restaurant was able to keep him stocked with prime steaks and fresh Italian peppers, which were smuggled into the prison inside loaves of bread. The prison guards ate regularly at Paoli's, courtesy of Mickey.

The truth of the matter concerning cuisine was that the prison chef would cook whatever the big boys in the house wanted, including Kosher corned beef on Mickey Cohen Day. Alcatraz had had a history of prison riots because of the substandard food. But during Mickey's stay, the cuisine included salads, fruit, multiple entrees, and desserts. That was the only good news.

JFK and RFK knew that Mickey needed politicians to support his early release. The Kennedys thought that he would cooperate if they dangled opportunities to leave. In October 1962, the brothers pressured him to spill whatever else he knew about Nixon, whose association with Mickey the Democrats naturally loved. Others like Adlai Stevenson had tried to get more of the Nixon story years earlier, but Mickey initially stood by his mixed morals: it would have been ratting on Nixon. Overall, he maintained a pragmatic rationale; he couldn't have given a damn about Nixon or any politician, and described him years later, "like the newspapers stigmatized him...a used-car salesman or a three-card monte dealer...a hustler." All he ever needed from any politician was "the best of what you've got going."

Democratic liberal politician Governor Pat Brown, who had been campaigning early for the 1962 election, contacted Mickey in prison. Brown was up for re-election in California against recently defeated presidential candidate Nixon. JFK personally sent Chief Deputy Attorney General Richard R. Rogan to take Mickey's statement, as Brown's emissary.

The politicians had Mickey in a tight spot; he told them more of what they wanted to hear, that he and many others like him had supported Nixon for years. He sent word to his brother Harry in Las Vegas to help Brown, whose chances looked good, with the election. The behind-bars lobbyist appeared to be lining up an early release, and through, of all people, the Kennedy Democratic machine.

It certainly didn't hurt Brown when Drew Pearson received Mickey's support to write articles on Nixon's mob connections, particularly the fundraiser at the Knickerbocker Hotel.[2] Pearson's

"Washington Merry-Go-Round" column stayed with the Cohen-Nixon story for years, despite Nixon's purported friendship with Mickey. Pearson was a consistent Nixon basher, not only because of the conservative views expressed in "Washington Merry-Go-Round," but also because of Nixon's egregious and corrupt leanings.[3]

The IRS followed through and sued Mickey on December 26. U.S. Attorney Francis C. Whelan pursued the uncollected taxes dating back to 1945—$374,476.38, including interest.

Mickey moved from decayed Alcatraz[4] to Atlanta on February 27, 1963, where his predecessor by four years was Mafia family boss Vito Genovese (Don Vito). Vito had had a job in the electric shop; it would become Mickey's. He also gave some of his personal belongings to Mickey, including a hot plate and a radio. Mickey was proud to take over for Vito, who ran his mob from his cell in Atlanta and who saw to it that

Mickey received special attention, including access to a private shower. Mickey bought all the comforts possible with extra cash and cigarettes.

Attorney General Robert F. Kennedy was not satisfied with Mickey's assistance, and decided to make the most of his incarceration before his first parole date. He wanted extensive information about syndicated crime, and hoped to make Mickey an informant. Early in Mickey's Atlanta stay, Kennedy personally traveled to the prison to intimidate him, unexpectedly cornering him when he was about to shower.

With five reporters all holding cameras, Kennedy confronted nude Mickey and asked, "How the hell are ya gonna live fifteen years in this goddamn chicken coop?"

Mickey replied, "...Don't worry about me."

Kennedy all but told him he was a free man, if only he would "be a little cooperative."

Mickey declined to cooperate, covered himself with a towel, and moved toward the shower, again a *stand-up guy*. He was not a stoolie and did not regard Kennedy as a trustworthy confidant, but as an enemy.

RFK had made many enemies, and some like Jimmy Hoffa and Carlos Marcello plotted his demise. Marcello had also discussed the idea to murder JFK, in order to neutralize RFK's activities against organized crime.[5]

After rebuffing Kennedy, Mickey dug in for a long haul. Unlike Marcello on the outside, Mickey never publicly swore vengeance against RFK, who relentlessly pursued Marcello through deportation attempts and more McClellan hearings.

On Wednesday, August 14, 1963, a dramatic event changed fifty-year-plus Mickey's life forever. While he was watching the midday news, unstable fellow convict Berl Estes McDonald hit Mickey on the head with a three-foot, lead conduit pipe. McDonald would have had to scale a twelve-foot wall in the yard, an obvious breach of prison security, to reach Mickey.

The medical report included a left homonymous hemangioma field defect, triplegia involving left arms and legs, a compound comminuted depressed skull fracture with a three-centimeter depression, and brain damage that required the removal of thirty grams of macerated tissue from the right superior parietal region.

The neurosurgeon who relieved the pressure on Mickey's brain reported that his survival was in limbo for forty-eight hours. His blood pressure and pulse soon stabilized, and his respiration returned to normal. He could have easily died. He was unconscious for six hours after the beating, and thereafter mentally alert. The injury was serious enough to warrant surgery to implant a steel plate, which doctors initially held in abeyance pending his recuperation, but subsequently placed.

A week after the incident, medical officer Dr. Richard Yocum told Mickey's girlfriend Sandy Hagen, "It's a little bit early to assess any permanent damage. He's doing well, considering the damage that was done." He said that Mickey had weakness in the left arm, and some leg paralysis, but none of the symptoms were indicators of permanent damage. Although not reported by the doctor, Mickey had limited use of his right hand.

Investigators represented that McDonald acted independently, and charged him with assault with intent to murder. He had a history of violent acts against prisoners, and yet authorities cut his now fifty-year sentence down to twenty-five years at the time of the incident, resulting in little reprisal for his actions.[6]

Warden David M. Heritage tried to minimize Mickey's condition by publicly stating that he had only a compound depressed fracture. He stated that Mickey provoked McDonald during an argument in the prison shop, adding that the mob was not connected.

Heritage told reporters, "It was a personal disagreement between two prisoners."

McDonald later apologized for his actions and made sure that Mickey received the message. Mickey remained puzzled as to why inmates like McDonald had access to the general prison population instead of being isolated in special sections for the mentally unstable. He was not buying the authority's explanation that McDonald had gone to great lengths to reach his section of the prison.

On October 2, 1963, Mickey left for a federal medical prison in Springfield, Missouri, where he would undergo more

extensive brain surgery. After the operation, he was unable to walk and lost the
use of one arm. Doctors suspected he
would never regain total use of his legs.
His recuperation was slow, and began with
daily four-hour physical therapy sessions
at General Hospital in Los Angeles, where
he had a twenty-four hour guard. When he
returned to Springfield medical prison, he
spent his first eleven months in
deadlock—completely isolated from the
prison population. The director of the
clinic, Dr. De Armond Moore wanted to be
certain that no further harm came to him.
Mickey didn't agree with the
recommendation, but had little choice in
the matter.

When he was feeling better, he engaged
Melvin Belli to initiate a lawsuit against
the government over the beating incident,
which Mickey insisted was preventable.
This marked the beginning of his long-
standing interest in prison reform.[7]

Many conspiracy theorists have linked Mickey and the mob to the Kennedy assassination of November 22, 1963, despite the timing of the McDonald attack and his recuperation. Money to help the mob cause was supposedly pouring in from unlikely sources, like California, where wealthy ranchers were angry with JFK for helping the farm workers. Even Robert Kennedy, without labeling the mob's role, later told Arthur Schlesinger, Jr., in New York's famous hamburger joint P. J. Clarke's, that the Warren Report "was a poor job." Gerald Posner wrote in his book *Case Closed*, as many believe today, that the JFK assassination has only one conclusion: one shooter, one bullet, no conspiracy.

Nevertheless, a few roads led to Mickey. Jim Garrison's investigation, Frank Mankiewicz's connecting JFK assassin Lee Harvey Oswald to David Ferrie/Ferret Man, and Ferrie's connection to Jack Ruby, Carlos Marcello, and Mickey all raised eyebrows. Author Michael Collins Piper cites Ferrie's employment from Carlos Marcello in New Orleans, down the hall from Jim Braden. Dallas, the city where the assassination took place, was a Marcello stronghold, controlled by boss Joseph Civello.[8] Author Piper, no friend to the Anti-Defamation League, loves to involve the Jewish mob, Israeli lobby, and even the Mossad in his theories on JFK's assassination.

Mickey's relationship to Marcello looms large on the list of guilt by association. He had become a player on the national scene, partly through Marcello, who had connections all the way up to the CIA; they asked his advice on how to assassinate Castro.

After Jack Ruby shot Lee Harvey Oswald, many Americans felt that he had done the right thing; he was a great citizen; he got the SOB who killed our president. They could not have been more wrong about Ruby's character, and were in

the dark about his mob background,
relationship to Mickey, and abusive style.[9]
FBI agents interviewed Mickey and Ruby's
girlfriend Candy Barr twelve hours after
Ruby shot Oswald.

The level of Mickey's involvement is a
connect-the-dots insinuation. Some
conspiracy mavens, like author and former
detective Gary Wean, can't get enough of
the fact that Ruby and Mickey were both
Jewish. Wean had access to all the
information that the local police and
prosecutors knew about old friends Mickey
and Ruby.

Conspiracy theorists also thrive when
they review the fact that famous defense
attorney and Mickey buddy Melvin Belli
jumped in so fast to represent Ruby after
he had killed assassin Oswald. To defend
him, Belli accepted a paltry $25,000 fee,
and hoped to make up the difference on
the book rights.

He likened Ruby to Mickey. "If you had
to pick Cohen up to drive him to the court

at 8:30, he would have to start getting himself ready at 5:30. Ruby was the same type."

Belli also referred to Ruby as "a junior version of Mickey Cohen." Ruby loved to name drop Mickey.

Throw in Menachem Begin again, and the Jewish plot thickens. The fact that Belli, Mickey, and Begin met occasionally to discuss how to cope with the Kennedy administration's foreign policy makes for lively speculation and further connections. Gary Wean, whose writing about Mickey sounded anti-Semitic, wrote, "[My partner] and I'd been watching Mickey Cohen from a distance. We knew he was up to something out of the ordinary. He spent a lot of time with a weird-looking little guy at the Beverly Wilshire Hotel lunch counter and drug store area." The little guy turned out to be Menachem Begin. Wean employed a Yiddish-speaking spy to find out what the two had discussed. Much of it had to do with Cuba, military operations, and the Kennedys. Both men despised JFK's appropriations for the "crazy Peace Corps." After the meeting, the two men adjourned to the home of Melvin Belli.

Utilizing an objective approach, even Jonathan Mark, associate editor of the *Jewish Week,* wrote, "Yes, Jack Ruby did kill JFK's assassin, Lee Harvey Oswald, and as far back as Lenny Bruce Jews have wondered whether Ruby's Jewishness had anything to do with it. It may have been a motive, after all." The Ruby photo caption raises the old question, "Jack Ruby: Did he have a 'Jewish reason' for killing Lee Harvey Oswald?" At the simplest level, some questioned if Ruby's motivation was to get even for the loss of JFK, whom, he felt, had done a great deal for Israel.

Mark mentions that Hugh Aynesworth of the *Washington Times* saw Ruby only five minutes before the assassination. Ruby was doing his schmooze act at the *Dallas Morning News,* and complained about an unsigned, black-bordered ad that attacked Kennedy: JFK—WANTED FOR TREASON. Ruby called the ad "dirty."

He later surmised that authorities could connect him to the assassination since Bernard Weissman, an associate of his, had placed the ad. Ruby told his sister that he had to leave Dallas because he could "never live this down." Aynesworth said that Ruby "connected [the unfolding events] to the fact that he and Weissman both were Jews." All media coverage dropped the name "Rubenstein" after the first go 'round surrounding Oswald's death, the opposite of standard reporting procedures. Instead of his proper name, Jack Rubenstein would become only "Ruby."

Author David Scheim expounded on the Ruby links: "It turned out that 'Jim Braden' was a changed name... Eugene Hale Brading had in fact used four other aliases...was checked through the California Department of Motor Vehicles."

Brading was loitering around Dealey Plaza in Dallas when authorities took him into custody the day of the JFK assassination. He had stayed at the mob hangout Cabana Motel in Dallas the day before the assassination. Ruby had stopped at the hotel around midnight. Both of them visited the H. L. Hunt Oil Company in Dallas at approximately the same time the afternoon before the assassination. Brading worked as a courier for Meyer Lansky, and was an original member of the Lansky-financed La Costa Country Club.

Brading's connections in the California underworld led to Mickey. He was close to Jimmy Fratianno, Harold "Happy" Meltzer, and Joe Sica, all with strong ties to Mickey. Another link is Al Gruber, also a Mickey associate. Ruby contacted Gruber right after the JFK assassination.

The conspiracy books cite multiple connections between Lansky's people, Carlos Marcello, and Mickey's circle. Mickey was undoubtedly Lansky's West

Coast representative. Lansky biographer Hank Messick described Mickey as Lansky's "eyes and ears," and after Bugsy's death continued to rely on him directly for information, utilizing couriers like Brading. While Ruby knew Mickey and Lansky, Mickey's day-to-day knowledge of Ruby's activities surrounding JFK is pure speculation, but possible. Some of Ruby's own comments confused observers, making his motives and connections impossible to nail down. In his memoir, Mickey wisely avoided mentioning Ruby. Michael Collins Piper in *Final Judgment* felt that Mickey's role was more significant: "Cohen—who was one of Jack Ruby's idols—apparently had a direct hand in the assassination conspiracy and the subsequent cover-up." Further, he suggested an alternative motive for the alleged murder of Marilyn Monroe: if she had publicly revealed how Mickey had used her to get information on JFK's Israeli foreign policy, the exposure of

Israel's uneasiness with JFK would have caused catastrophic political consequences here and abroad.

Local attention did not diminish while Mickey was in prison. The IRS arranged to sell his jewelry that agents had confiscated against his back taxes. Newspapers advertised the public auction, set for December 18, 1963. Jeweler Jack Fuerst, 222 W. 5th St., authenticated the unique forty-three-piece collection, and handled the sale. LaVonne's nearly thirteen-carat diamond ring was the cornerstone of the collection. Mickey's solid gold key chain, diamond-studded and sapphire cuff links, tie tack made of two gold dice with diamonds and rubies for the spots, gold his-and-her pen set, and a gold house key were all part of the expensive and gaudy jewels. Mickey had a collection of watches to match every color suit. Even the face of the watch coordinated with each ornate wristband. The IRS expected that the auction would fetch a minimum of $50,000. Fuerst mentioned to reporters that only one fake diamond existed. Mickey had given the kitschy bauble to stripper girlfriend Candy Barr in 1959. After sealed bids, IRS agents recorded sales of $20,000.

Paul Coates offered one of the best newspaper assessments of Mickey's complex life and morality in a piece for the *Los Angeles Times* on December 27, 1963. The KTTV Channel 11 television reporter spoke in detail about Mickey's generosity, wry humor, and interest in love.

He recalled the Pearson beating episode: "It was an incredible scene beyond, even, the imagination of Damon Runyon."

A letter to a nurse that Mickey knew in Los Angeles revealed yet another side of his multifaceted makeup. He wrote her because he was unable to keep a Christmas package that she had sent him during his prison stay.

I received your always most appreciated letter... I was very pleased that you spoke with my sis.... You know it is not easy enough to tell one not to become bitter or not to become hateful. But the thing is, how to tell one how to avoid becoming that way... it is a terrible thing when you read about some young fellows who just got released from a place like I'm in, and soon after they're out, they kill a police officer. If you could witness, as I have, the embittered frame of minds of some of these persons just before they are released to live in the free world... You would be shocked and disturbed at some of the statements made to me by some of these soon-to-be-released prisoners...many just mouth off to make an impression on me...

About six weeks into 1964, Jack Dahlstrum of Los Angeles, Melvin Belli of San Francisco (still working on Jack Ruby's case), J. Victor Candy, Jr., of

Nashville, and William B. Paul of Atlanta had filed a suit against the federal government for $10,000,000. The more than twenty-page civil action filing was extensive and very clear: the government had failed to keep Mickey safe in prison. The lawyers had done their homework; they knew every inch of the penitentiary and utilized schematics to make their case. The landmark complaint accused the penitentiary of operating "in a negligent and careless manner," resulting in Mickey's leg paralysis and brain damage. Attorneys asked for loss of income damages, a difficult figure to estimate, particularly based on Mickey's tax trial statistics.

On March 12, Mickey requested a medical parole. He wrote the document himself, and attorney A. L. Wirin delivered the biographical twelve-page handwritten plea to the court, supported by signatures of 305 respected citizens.

Mickey excused his chosen profession in the request: "...in those days was looked upon as being a normal process for an unschooled and uneducated young boy who had to earn money to eat, and to help feed his loved ones."

Wirin sent copies of the documents to pardon attorney Reed Cozart, who worked for the Department of Justice and who would recommend and forward the material to Attorney General Robert F. Kennedy with copies to President Lyndon Johnson.

This go 'round would prove futile. Mickey's first scheduled parole date was still December 1966.

Ben Hecht died April 19, 1964, but not before the British vilified him for his Irgun activities. Sidney Zion spoke of the irony: "Thus Ben Hecht became the first blacklisted Hollywood writer. And by the goddamn English, at that."[10]

Mickey added another lawsuit for $1,000,000 against the government of

Atlanta, Georgia, under the Federal Tort Claim Act.

Less than a year later, he would receive a break from prison life. He returned to Los Angeles on a Friday in late February 1965. Federal Judge Gus Solomon, brought in from Portland as a substitute, had signed a court order to allow Mickey to attend the government trial for the more than two-year-old tax case. Attorney Jack Dahlstrum insisted that Mickey be present as a witness at the March 15 court battle.

His method of travel and subsequent treatment in Los Angeles indicated that his power had not substantially diminished. His twin-engine Beechcraft plane touched down at a private landing pad owned by AiResearch Corporation, within the confines of Los Angeles International Airport. The *Los Angeles Times* remarked that the scene resembled a "secret mission" of "a high government official."

An officer of the corporation had ordered the plane for Mickey, and the company provided an extensive number of security guards, who had instructions to keep the press onslaught away from him. He shuffled to the waiting station wagon with the aid of a cane.

He had a "hotel reservation" at the prison ward in General Hospital, including around the clock guards. Only attorneys and family could visit.

Dahlstrum arranged a press conference on March 2 to drum up sympathy for broken-man Mickey. He discussed Mickey's memory loss, which attorneys attributed to his attack. Reporters questioned the extent of his impairment, and naturally wondered about the accuracy of his answers during any trial.

Two days before the tax trial, a new three-column Paul Coates piece on Mickey appeared in the sympathetic *Los Angeles Times.*

Coates began with, "Mickey Cohen, the banty rooster who once strutted the walks of the Sunset Strip..."

Dahlstrum had told Coates about the shoddy prison conditions and treatment and described the hospital as a place filled with "dangerous psychotics." Mickey never fully recovered from the savage beating and was in pitiful condition. He, who avoided the television room, still wondered if he had ever seen McDonald before the beating, while authorities refused to show him his assailant's picture. He was at one time totally paralyzed, permanently lost his left field of vision in both eyes, lost the use of one arm, still had paralysis in both legs, and had a "silver" plate in his skull.

Dahlstrum complained: "Until they brought him here for this tax suit, he hadn't been out in the open air for 18 months. They're afraid to let him out in the yard. He hasn't been allowed to attend a movie or religious service in that time."

The reporter pleaded the obvious. "I wouldn't argue that he should not do his time...as a simple matter of humanity, I do not think he should be made to do it in a prison where it might cost him his life." Mickey had received the rawest of deals. Officials refused a transfer to Terminal Island at the ship dock in San Pedro closer to his family. The medical staff at the Springfield penitentiary could no longer improve his condition.

He arrived for his IRS tax trial in a neat suit, and walked with the aid of a black twisted cane. In order to protect his relatives, who had a controlling interest in his greenhouse, he had signed a waiver under duress in 1956 upon advice of attorney Paul Caruso and pressure from IRS agent Peter R. Bertoglio, who threatened foreclosure on several properties.

After a visit by a U.S. attorney, Caruso denied that he had planned to support Dahlstrum's case. Angry Judge Solomon

challenged Dahlsturm's perjury implica-
tions regarding Caruso, denying his move
for dismissal because of Caruso's flip-flop.

Assistant U.S. Attorney James S. Bay
continued with the case against Mickey,
despite acknowledging that he held no
assets. That was the end of the witness
list.

Mickey waited at the prison hospital
until March 24 for Judge Solomon's
reserved decision. The judge ruled against
him, allowed him a minuscule credit for
$15,000 worth of seized property, and
sent him back to Springfield.

Mickey idol Owney Madden died on April
24, 1965, in a Hot Springs, Arkansas,
hospital. Chief Parker finally retired in
1965, and died the next year.

The FBI continued to keep a close watch
on Mickey, despite his debilitating
episode. Agents were convinced that he
was still running his operations on the
outside, and they were desperate to
incriminate him. FBI guru Hoover had

reported only sixty-five gambling and racketeering convictions, with few leaders. Many government officials, politicians, police, and agents represented then and now that Mickey was not a significant national player. The resultant FBI effort became one of the most costly and ludicrous reportages in the history of the federal agency.

Brother Harry became the focus of the FBI for the next two years. He confessed to smuggling contraband to Mickey—all necessities to keep his life civil.

Mickey's big drug score in prison was twenty Dristan inhalers. The FBI raided the prison on July 12, 1965, but recovered only ten of the inhalers, one can of vegetable beef soup, one two-ounce jar of Brilliantine (hair tonic), a jar of antipasto, a jar of Aqua Velva, and six slices of rye bread.

The FBI continued to watch his every move, despite acknowledging that he did not take drugs. His treatment smacked of personal vendettas; he had alienated himself from so many high-ranking officials that his political power had substantially diminished; the FBI harassed him unmercifully.

They discovered that Harry had bribed a nurse with $100 to provide additional food and toilet articles for his brother.

The prison nurse cracked under pressure from FBI agents: "...I was contacted by Mickey Cohen...to get him some tea that had lemon and sugar in it. I told him he could get tea here but said it did not have lemon in it. He kept asking me... I brought him a couple of packages of tea." Then all hell broke loose. "Cohen thanked me for it and he asked me for something else, probably salami, mustard or something to eat... I continued bringing him pretty much the same items including herring and Jewish salami."

The nurse confessed to other atrocities like mailing letters for Mickey, and making phone calls to Harry.

The FBI contraband investigation spread to New York; Patterson, New Jersey; and Springfield, Missouri. Five nurses and three senior officers at the prison got into the act. A whopping two hundred bucks were involved. The livid FBI interviewed banks and traced money orders.

Mickey's attorneys told him not to talk to the FBI, who advised him of his rights in accordance with new policy: "...any statements he did make could be used against him in a court of law." During a second brief, illogical meeting, Mickey told the agents that he would be stupid to eat food that he found in his room.

This slapstick epidemic of prison violations produced more non-commissary items on January 14, 1966. The new list of niceties included a six-ounce jar of Mr. Mustard. Five new packages of Nestea ice tea mix. A jar of Lipton ice tea mix. A twelve-ounce jar of Torrido brand chili peppers. A Fanci-Food three-ounce jar of hot mustard. Two glass jars of relish, and horseradish.

The FBI found a small bottle of yellow Sominex pills. Unlike the commercial, there would be no "Take Sominex tonight, and sleep, sleep, sleep" for Mickey. Somebody tipped off the agents about a roll of meat and two non-government-issue rolls of pepperoni in the dark room.

They assigned a fulltime undercover agent to keep an eye on him. On January 27, 1966, the warden cooperated in a crackdown on the entire prison population. The only confessions were chewing gum. An interviewee ratted Mickey out. The prison-striped clotheshorse had four or five pairs of fancy pajamas. He liked Czech broadcloth, which the FBI mentioned was very hard to get— they meant in general, not in prison.

The big casino closer: the Cohen brothers were after fresh linens and shower-related items. Case closed! For the moment.

While many show-business people stuck by Mickey during this prison stay, the majority of people, including the throngs of politicians and police who missed the payroll money, slowly wrote him off. The celebrity mail trickled in. Journalists had less to say about him since he was no longer in the public eye. Many smaller articles focused on anything remotely related to him or his associates.

The FBI still watched his mail with interest. Agents labeled one love letter "obscene." Very likely, Sandy Hagen sent these excerpts. Agents blacked out the affectionate terms, greeting, and signature:

...I keep thinking of you constantly—what do you look like—I'm so afraid I won't even recognize you...am I dreaming or being hopeful—at times I start thinking—asking myself how many weeks—days—then I get a cold chill—I'm so afraid—everyone tells me to think positive—I'm...praying-begging God—for this one favor-a chance to bring you home to make you well...the few years that we have left—will we enjoy them somewhat... I'm so sick at heart—not having been able to visit you—see you—..."

Mickey received extensive letters from friends and relatives, some from comedian Joey Bishop. People supplied narratives about life on the outside, and allowed Mickey to envision the ordinary things that might help a prisoner look toward the future.

Mickey's devoted sister, likely Pauline or Lillian, wrote descriptive and dramatic letters:

...I must take my hat off to you for what you once told me about how to handle all people and supposed to be friends when you do anyone a favor, to make them pay for it thru the nose and

have no mercy for anyone, money wise
when they come to you for a favor...guys
who were former pals and I grew up with,
who completely play the cold shoulder...

Sister Rose, an FBI creation, perhaps
Mickey's sister-in-law, ran a children's
apparel store, although they blackened the
signature on the letter. The lengthy letters
cover extensive details of his sister's
business relationship with him, plus
discussions with attorneys, and how
generally to help him.

On January 25, 1966, authorities
released Mickey to travel to Atlanta
regarding his $10,000,000 suit against the
government. On trips like this, he would
have to pay off between fifteen and
twenty-five hundred dollars to support the
extra prison guard entourage.

U.S. District Judge Sidney O. Smith, Jr.,
listened to juryless arguments over a two-
day period, January 31 and February 1.

In court, when federal marshals tried to assist a hobbled Mickey, he told them, "I'm OK, leave me alone."

Attorneys for the government kept him on the stand for over one hour.

Mickey told Judge Sidney Smith, "I would be willing to do anything to be able to walk again."

The government still tried to establish that the prison had reasonable security measures, and that guards had control over the inmates. Attorneys conceded that Mickey's assailant McDonald was not of sound mind. Testimony revealed that he had escaped into the exercise yard from a separate maximum-security area, traveled over 500 feet, and then clubbed Mickey. He was incapable of standing trial.

Judge Smith had no problem chastising the penitentiary staff. The judge deemed Mickey permanently disabled, lame, and crippled for life. However, the judge deferred his verdict.

When Mickey returned to prison, the FBI did not let up. They traced money from cities all over the country to the prison.

The pulled Mickey's brother Harry in for further questioning about letter writing, money orders, and telephone calls.

Toward the end of March, Mickey ultimately received a judgment against the government for only $110,000, due upon his release.

Despite government objections, Russian-born Allen Smiley, who had shown Bugsy to his last seat, received his United States citizenship in July. West Hollywood resident Smiley said that he was in the oil business, and proud of his recent honor.

The persistent FBI had to take a breather in July, since an airline strike halted their peripatetic trips to interview witnesses.

They suffered a rare glimpse into reality during September 1966: "Within the prison Mickey Cohen is well regarded and

respected by many of the inmate popu-
lace... As the Bureau is aware he is
paralyzed from the waist down and
incapable of physical harm to anyone in
his present condition..." The same report
discussed the work-release program, and
stated that no one previously released
under the program had fled.

Mickey was outliving many of his
enemies. After a one-year illness, fifty-
seven-year-old Captain James Hamilton,
who had collected a judgment in the libel
and slander suit against Mickey and ABC,
died on November 7. On November 30,
1966, the Federal Parole Board denied his
current request for release. It offered no
reason for the decision, and refusal to offer
him work programs. Fans followed the two-
weak media coverage.

Harry Cohen's only recourse was to
publicize Mickey's predicament. On
December 9, Los Angeles KLAC radio
interviewed him. He candidly told
Mickey's public about prison

homosexuality, harassment, horrible medical care, and brutality.

On January 31, 1967, Mattie Capone died. Few attended the service in which two reporters covering the funeral filled in as pallbearers.

Prison authorities allowed Mickey to visit the Kaiser Foundation Hospital to see his eighty-two-year-old mother Fanny, who had suffered a heart attack. Mickey returned to prison on February 5.

On May 21, he attended his mother's funeral. He needed assistance to stand, and used a cane to steady himself. He was tired, but refused his wheelchair. He buried Mrs. Fanny Friedman at Hillside Memorial Park cemetery, known as the resting place of the stars.

Despite his poor health, he could not ascertain a release based on his medical condition.

On May 31, the FBI still wondered: should they prosecute the nurse or only Mickey?

Finally! Wonderful news for taxpayers. January 5, 1968, Assistant United States Attorney Anthony P. Nugent, Jr., confirmed: "...reported that in view of the age of the proposed case against Mickey Cohen as well as other problems....decline prosecution."

Nevertheless, Mickey was in terrible physical condition, and still in prison. In 1968, his brother Harry[11] appealed to Attorney General Ramsey Clark:

> ...My brother's "life" is in grave danger...attempt to murder him by "poisoning him." ...capsules prescribed by the U.S. Medical Center... We his family are mighty worried... My brother was sentenced as a healthy perfect physical specimen...today is a hopeless cripple.

Harry's list of Mickey's ailments included asthma and ulcers. He asserted that Mickey's punishment was cruel and unusual, and that maybe Robert Kennedy had been behind his extensive and inflexible sentence. He asked for leniency, and pointed out that Mickey had already served half of his sentence. His request for Mickey's medical parole had a legitimate basis. Success would have come more easily to a less celebrated and notorious inmate.

The FBI stated that Harry had offered to "buy" Mickey's release, and also noted, "He [Harry] claims that the inmates are treated like animals, that he is in the process of preparing a book concerning the alleged cruel, inhuman care, violation of human dignity and civil rights."

In a separate letter to Director Hoover, Harry pleaded, "...even you would be shocked and amazed at some of the goings on...inhumane, sadistic, etc... His large family never condoned his escapades, and past life and activities, however, he is my baby brother and I am concerned." He made it clear to Hoover that many less deserving inmates had received parole through payoffs and fixes. He got nowhere with the FBI or anyone else.

During 1968, Nick Licata took the reigns of the Italian mob, and did not fair much better than his predecessors Frank DeSimone and Jack Dragna.

When Sirhan Sirhan assassinated Robert Kennedy on June 5, 1968, conspiracy theories related to Mickey immediately sprung up. The shooting occurred in the Ambassador Hotel—always a Mickey stronghold. The existing theories on the RFK assassination are detailed and widespread, and even suggest that Los Angeles was the target city because Mickey could more easily order and control the set-up.

The simplest conspiracy theory makes Sirhan the fall guy, and identifies a security officer—not Sirhan—firing and hitting Kennedy, since the fatal bullets came from close range, closer than the two to three feet some people reported as Sirhan's position.

RFK conspiracy theorists mention Mickey's name frequently because his motive was obvious and simple: if Kennedy became president, Mickey could kiss the rest of his own life goodbye. He had always been an RFK priority, years before his brother's assassination. After JFK's death, Robert Kennedy did somewhat reduce his focus on Mickey.

According to author John Davis, it is impossible not to consider the obvious: Hoffa, Marcello, and Mickey all would benefit from a "plot to murder the man who, while serving as attorney general, had ordered J. Edgar Hoover to go after Jimmy Hoffa, Carlos Marcello, and Mickey Cohen." Even prison did not stop Hoffa from hatching a plan to kill RFK with the help of Marcello and Carmine Galante, underboss of the New York Bonanno crime family.

Kennedy was particularly disturbed by Mickey's history of extortion and pimping; it was no secret that he controlled movie stars through blackmail. As president, Kennedy would have had the familiar Department of Justice at his disposal; it could have had a field day with Mickey, and blocked his release.

Conspiracy mavens vigorously stir the pot when it comes to assassin Sirhan's connections to Mickey, the mob, and Hollywood. He worked at the Santa Anita racetrack, where Mickey's organization had pervasive influence. Sirhan, who attended Pasadena's John Muir High School and Pasadena City College, was never the extreme Arab activist as painted by the media. He mistook our pop-culture to be the real America, as did many foreigners implanted in Hollywood. His acquaintances described him as very much American; he loved to make a buck, and shunned anything Arab—cuisine, garb, etc. He performed grooming and exercise work around the stables, but like other track bums, his salary was hardly enough to pay his gambling debts, making him beholden to the mob. An impressionable Arab-Palestinian exercise boy would have been a likely choice by someone interested in igniting the smoldering differences surrounding the political struggle for Israeli survival. Nevertheless, Sirhan was schooled on the Arab warrior Saladin, who expelled unwanted crusaders from Jerusalem, and weaned on typical anti-American, anti-Semitic, and pro Palestinian sentiments.

The conspiracy theory rolls on with the *I Love Lucy* connection. Sirhan was friends with well-known horse trainer Frank Donneroumas, who introduced him to Desi Arnaz, who had a fancy horse-breeding ranch in Corona, where Sirhan worked. Arnaz was always on good terms with Mickey, as well as with Sinatra, despite the embellished public confrontation over *The Untouchables* television show.

Donneroumas was former criminal Henry Ramistella, a middle management racketeer from New Jersey who disappeared west after being banned from the East Coast tracks. FBI investigations linked Ramistella, Sirhan, and Arnaz to Mickey.

Another conspiracy angle involves Richard Nixon. Carlos Marcello and Mickey were always supporters of Nixon, despite Mickey playing both sides of the fence in the 1962 California gubernatorial election. Marcello had donated $500,000 to Nixon's 1960 loss to JFK. Senate investigator Walter Sheridan understood the Jewish mob's likewise interest in Nixon: "If you were Meyer, who would you invest your money in? Some politician named Clams Linguini? Or a nice Protestant boy from Whittier, California?" With RFK gone, Nixon would likely win the presidency, assuring mobsters access to the White House.[12]

Murray Chotiner, who was still one of Nixon's closest allies, tried to distance himself from Mickey. He had always stayed on good terms with Mickey since he represented the interests of East Coast syndicate bosses like Costello and Meyer Lansky.[13]

Chotiner threatened to sue columnist Pearson if he continued to play up Mickey's relationship with him and Nixon. He called Mickey to intervene. Mickey did call Pearson and asked him to focus on other stories. Chotiner dropped all charges against Pearson.

Mickey's failed attempts for release, his prison treatment, and the silly FBI scrutiny had more to do with his political enemies than any public outcry to see justice served. Since his power and influence had reached the highest levels, many people associated him with high crime against America, things that went way beyond the scope of his local operations. If any of the implied conspiracy allegations were true, then his extensive punishment may have been appropriate, but his trial and subsequent incarceration had been solely for a tax law violation.

His role in American politics was that of a businessman in a national company that needed a lobby in Washington, but his heart really wasn't in his political success and its trappings. His passion was with Hollywood, and his deeply personal need to tell his own story, rather than someone else's. Watching others rise on the national scene did not appeal to him as much as his own celebrity needs.

4.

ᶠor many years, the police in Beverly Hills, Hollywood, and greater Los Angeles had denied the existence of the Mafia or any Mafia-like organization that operated within shopping distance of trendy Rodeo Drive or Sunset Boulevard. In June 1967, Attorney General Thomas C. Lynch of California broke the "startling" news. "Our state has become the favorite investment area of the veiled finance committee of organized crime." Author Ed Reid listed the discoveries:

...hidden interests on state licenses: the intrusion of criminal cartelists into our sensitive world of finance; the layoff of huge sports bets into the Los Angeles area; loan sharking and the reported moves of the remnants of the old Mickey Cohen mob to control it.

The same year that Lynch started his late war on crime, contrarians like U.S. Deputy Attorney General Warren M. Christopher, who later became secretary of state under President Bill Clinton, made statements about the lack of organized crime in California. Organized crime did not exist "because of the quality, honesty, and integrity" of our law enforcement agencies. He did not believe that anyone involved with crime in California had anything to do with national or secret organizations. Reid was critical of the blanket appraisal: "But perhaps Christopher was the victim of ignorance." More realistically, Christopher had followed the pattern established years earlier by FBI deity J. Edgar Hoover.

The *New York Observer* writer Ron Rosenbaum's recent description of Hollywood may account for its having fallen easy prey to Mickey and the mob for so many years: "Hollywood is our nation's head injury, the source of our spiritual retardation."

The export of pop-culture from Mickey's neighborhood always took a front seat to any serious anti-crime activity. The country was regularly infused with news of Hollywood, and on its way to becoming a celebrity-driven society. More than one American pop icon, television guru, or minimally skilled actor would publicize their felonies that ranged from narcotics violations to stock swindles, and from sex offenses to murder, while most of their careers continued to soar.

Thanks to the inadvertent activities of peripatetic Mickey and his boys, the actual city of Hollywood would change dramatically. Mob-controlled illegal and posh conventional activities shifted west, to the newer and safer West Hollywood and Beverly Hills. It was no longer possible to see a movie star strolling along famous Hollywood and Vine; there was a much greater chance to see one on chichi Rodeo Drive. Regular Hollywood destinations of the prior decades evaporated. The last big Broadway department store had seen better days, and the posh Pig and Whistle restaurant, along with many other famous eateries, eventually lost its movie star-driven clientele. The local movie theaters had all but given up on Hollywood premieres, except the famous Grauman's Chinese, today the Mann and still a tourist trap.

The money shift west produced unmanageable crime in the vacated sections. The Hollywood vice squad had its hands full with pimps and drug addicts who had infiltrated the once innocent sightseers' haven, ironically no longer protected by more upscale organized crime. The corruption in the police department was still widespread; official cooperation ensured the success of criminals like Mickey in the volatile landscape.

Even while incarcerated in the late sixties and early seventies, Mickey maintained the dubious distinction of being the reigning king of rackets. His crews prolonged his hold on the business and warded off interlopers while he served the last few years of his second prison term. Police designed special units to help exclude organized crime from the more fashionable neighborhoods. That was fine with Mickey, who was more than willing to cooperate with the police to assist in keeping out the competitive undesirables. This perverse symbiotic relationship even allowed people like Mickey to help appoint police officials. The business-as-usual philosophy had perpetuated his operations, notwithstanding multiple public crusades by politicians seeking election to rid Hollywood and its bordering communities of organized crime.

While Mickey was in prison, *Life* profiled the success of Carlos Marcello in Louisiana, one of many examples of mobsters who avoided Kefauver, McClellan, RFK, and Hoover (who by then had completely turned his back on pursuing the bosses).[1]

During his absence, a reclusive gambling boss named Harry Gross tried to infiltrate Mickey's bookie operations. New Yorker Gross, convicted of bookmaking in 1950, had moved west and seized the opportunity created by Mickey's misfortune.

Al "Slick" Snyder, who suffered injuries in the Hooky Rothman slaying, became embroiled in the famous Friars Club card-cheating case. He refused to tell authorities anything about the installation of electronic cheating devices in the fabled Friars card room, peepholes in the ceiling and radio transmitters. Steven Crane's popular restaurant partner Al Mathes, who drove a white Rolls-Royce, was in on the take from the droves of Friars' pigeons.

When Nixon beat Humphrey in the 1968 presidential election, Mickey's hopes of early release diminished.[2] He had again agreed to let columnist Drew Pearson use the information about his relationship to Nixon in the hope that it would help elect Humphrey. Mickey's assessment of Nixon never changed over the years, and he told Pearson (who some say toppled Nixon), "...let's hope he isn't the same guy I knew as a rough hustler... I never had no idea that this guy Nixon could go anywhere..." He received no assistance from President Nixon, because this time Pearson published Mickey's entire statement.[3] He had been working directly with Pearson, who had the ear of then president Lyndon Johnson, whom Mickey swore double-crossed him on the parole issue. Governor Pat Brown in California likewise had stiffed Mickey on his medical parole

Florabel Muir died of a heart attack on April 27, 1970, at age eighty. Every obit mentioned the time that she was "shot in the hip" by a fusillade of bullets meant for Mickey, or some similar embellishment.

Mickey would not give up on early parole. The wounded warrior appeared before U.S. District Judge William H. Becker during July 1970. Listed as fifty-six, Mickey hobbled to the witness chair during his hearing for a writ of habeas corpus.

He described his life before McDonald hit him on the head. "...I was in charge of the tool room in the electric shop. It was a responsible position...my immediate supervisor said I was doing a good job... I was eligible... for meritorious good time." He had not received any time off for good behavior.

His attorneys asked for thirty-six days of credit for his first year of service at the penitentiary. Each additional year would bring sixty more days.

Mickey was pleased that his right hand had improved; he was now able to write, and told the judge that he was willing to work. He made certain to say that his sentence was "cruel and unusual punishment." He found the prison population difficult to bear because of his homophobia. He had frequent run-ins with prisoners whom he considered gay, and constantly complained to the guards and wardens. He was very vocal and called the prison "a male whorehouse," and refused to work with any man he suspected of being gay.

"I don't mix with no fags, no queers, no fruits," he said during interviews for good behavior sentence reduction.

Sexually panicked Mickey had had talks with Springfield Warden Dr. Pasquale J. Ciccone about the complications of his day-to-day existence, brought on by his response to many of the inmates whom he found repellent. The warden had encouraged him to be more accepting of

sexual diversity, at least intellectually—
something Mickey insisted was
impossible. (Of course, there are no
records of his sex life in prison. If anyone
had girls smuggled in at night by prison
guards, it was Mickey. Although, based on
reports by friends, he probably appreciated
his contraband steaks just as much as any
outside companionship.)

He referenced his doctors, who said that
release from prison tensions would
improve his health.

The worried judge had his assurance
that no harm would come to him on the
outside. "No, I have no fears... My heyday
is long past," said Mickey.

Judge Becker found Mickey's detention
lawful, and he remained in prison. His raw
deal continued.

In 1971, Meyer Lansky faced skimming
charges involving the now older Flamingo
Hotel. He would utilize Israel's law of
return, and eventually retire to the Tel
Aviv Dan Hotel, which he had built.

That same year Mickey's brother Harry appealed to Attorney General John Mitchell. In a pathetic and sad letter, he mentioned that someone had robbed Mickey on a Friday night when he had tried to attend a Sabbath service. Harry called the attacker "sadistic and bigoted." He asked Mitchell to use his influence to help Mickey retrieve his glasses from the thieves. Mickey claimed that it was a shakedown by a staff member, and not an inmate.

Harry contacted the American Civil Liberties Union for relief. He reiterated how the prison system had destroyed Mickey rather than rehabilitate him; he had never received the proper medical care, including physical therapy.

The matter was dumped in Hoover's lap, and he responded for everyone: "The copy of your letter to the Attorney General was received ... While I readily understand the concern...there does not appear to be a violation of Federal law within the investigative jurisdiction of the FBI." He forwarded Harry's complaints to the Bureau of Prisons. No action resulted from any of Harry's efforts.

Donald F. Bowler, the IRS agent who had headed the team that put Mickey away, retired from government service on March 26, 1971. He went to work for Intertel (International Intelligence), a company designed to keep the mob away from its clients, including mogul Howard Hughes.

The occasional story about Mickey's old gang made news. One example was on December 17: Seven-Dwarf Eli Lubin was indicted on mail fraud, related to a 1962 bond theft of twenty-eight $1,000 Series E savings bonds.

While Mickey's brother and others did their best to ascertain his release, he could do little more than wait. His Mandatory Release date was coming up soon.

5.

After years of requests, authorities announced that Mickey would be coming home on January 9, 1972, the Mandatory Release date, and the year FBI chief Hoover died. Only two months earlier, Riverside County sheriff's deputies had arrested fifty-eight-year-old interloper bookmaker Harry Gross, either ironically or conveniently for Mickey.

Mickey felt that his release should have come sooner, and prison authorities, who now wanted to appear sympathetic, publicly exaggerated the good behavior reports. Springfield Prison director Dr. Pasquale Ciccone claimed that Mickey had received the five years off his sentence for good behavior, although he would always adamantly deny it. Warden Ciccone released a statement that Mickey had been a "reasonably cooperative prisoner." Many reports claimed that he had been a favorite of wardens, guards, and inmates, despite his personal denials. Mickey insisted that no officials had gone out of their way to see that he received credit for good behavior. Authorities had denied him early release benefits while other prisoners consistently racked up reduced time. That bothered him more than any other element of prison life. Prisoners who were incarcerated for cold-blooded murder left quicker than he did.

Despite Mickey's model reputation and debilitated condition, countless FBI reports still ended with a warning to agents: he is likely armed and dangerous and he has killed in the past. Prison officials had ignored the FBI advice and had treated the celebrity gangster with a level of respect reserved for famous public figures.

Newspapers prepared the waiting public with a history of Mickey's career, including details about his varied business operations. Expressions like "bookie's bookie" and "successor to Benjamin 'Bugsy' Siegel" filled the papers across the country. Reporters reviewed Mickey's prison life, the bizarre attack, and subsequent rehabilitation. Ironically, just before his release, stripper Tempest Storm, admitting to age forty-three, received a one-year probation for not paying her taxes. (Folklore never ceased to remind us that the fiery redhead had her 44DD bosom insured with Lloyd's of London for $1,000,000.)

Harry arrived this time in a new 1972 white Cadillac El Dorado with Ohio license plates; some things never change. Mrs. Harry Cohen and associate Jim Smith were also in the car. Harry told reporters before Mickey appeared, "Mickey could leave earlier but he's taking three hours to get dressed. He's the same goof he's always been."

Authorities released Mickey from prison between nine-thirty and ten in the morning on January 6, 1972. He had received an early weekend release, as was the custom. He sometimes needed a three-footed cane for stability, and today he took advantage of its support. He held a supply of paper towels, so his hand would never touch the germy cane handle.

When interviewed for a filmed biography of Mickey, journalist Peter Noyes, choked with emotion, said "It was really sad to see him [Mickey] on camera... It was the end of the brash, cocky, little man, who cut such a path through Los Angeles."

Mickey left prison wearing a white T-shirt, an ill-fitting pair of pants rolled to the ankles, and a windbreaker. He looked rather ordinary, but not totally destroyed by his beating and prison stay.

He spat on the ground and said, "Pass my family." He explained later that as a child he would spit whenever he saw a dead cat or dog and invoke "pass my family," meaning "Death, pass my family."

He hobbled to the El Dorado and said, "To hell with this rotten joint," struggled into the car, sat quietly in the front seat, and stared straight ahead as Harry drove through the front gate of the U.S. Medical Center for Federal Prisoners. Newsmen from around the country congregated outside the gate, and packed the perimeter.

Mickey told reporters, one of whom was his nephew David Cohen, "I wanted to throw away the cane and start walking."

Harry told him that they would stop at a local motel in Springfield. Mickey remembered a little café called Hamby's across from the Springfield Federal Building nearby; he had eaten there during his appeal in July 1970. His later version recalls having Jim Smith bring the food to

the marshal's office during court recess.
Harry agreed to drive him to Hamby's so
he could have a piece of the chocolate pie
he remembered and now craved.

Reporters surrounded the boys at the
local café.

Within an hour, Mickey was on the
telephone with friends. One call was to
Sandy Hagen, in San Diego.

"Why are you crying?" he asked.

After the call, a reporter asked him if he
intended to see her.

"It's my intention to see her if she would
care to see me—you know." He would soon
encourage his girlfriend Sandy to marry.
She would take his advice, and eventually
had two children.

Mickey declared, "It's good to be free,
that's all," and refused to reveal any
detailed vacation plans, although he
mentioned Hot Springs, Arkansas, "to
wash the stink and stench of prison off
me." He had remained friends with Owney

Madden's family, who resided in Hot Springs.

He said that he planned to live in West Hollywood.

More relaxed, Mickey responded to questions about Bugsy. "I knew Bugs and I loved him. He was one of the best human beings I ever met in my life."

He devoured his piece of chocolate pie plus a large orange juice, ham, fried potatoes, and three fried eggs smothered in catsup.

The satiated free man referred to an $800,000 lien by the IRS and made it clear that the government wouldn't see a nickel. "Any money I can beg, borrow, or steal will have to go to correcting my physical condition."

He asserted, "I'm not a vicious man. I haven't been involved in any vicious incidents...even the days when I was considered a tough hoodlum. I had a strong sense of ethics."

Mickey now acknowledged that he had received eight hours of physical therapy each day, including weight lifting for his upper body, but had to return to substandard cell conditions— "unbelievably bad" solitary—most of his nights. He was convinced that McDonald had clubbed him because of his underworld connections.

His overall take on the medical facility was dismal, a "place where they sent the best-known Mafia types to die just like one of those elephant burial grounds I've read about," mentioning victims Vito Genovese and Jimmy "The Monk" Alegretti. Don Vito, as he liked to be called, died of a heart attack in prison, following a ten-year stay.

Los Angeles Times reporter Bryce Nelson observed, "He is still a quick conversationalist whose dark eyes flash and whose bushy gray eyebrows bristle when he describes the 'rotten, sadistic conditions in prison.'"

Mickey commented on his employment possibilities: "I've had my belly full of it [gambling]—I'm not that strong any more...in my day it was different. People look at those kinds of things different nowadays. What I want to do for the rest of my years is live them out as easily as I can."

After a manicure and haircut, fifty-eight-year-old Mickey hosted a party that night in Springfield, Missouri, at the aptly named Shady Inn. Another gala awaited him on his return to Los Angeles, where he would find that his world had changed substantially. Much of the old mob was gone. Sam LoCigno—who went to prison for the Whalen shooting—had died of a heart attack in Cleveland the previous year.

The movie hit of the year was *The Godfather*, an epic based on the Mario Puzo book, starring Marlon Brando, Al Pacino, and James Caan. Some New Yorkers said that the book was derivative of the actual lives of the Profaci crime syndicate, while others had different favorites. Surely, the singer Johnny Fontaine could be no one but Sinatra, and Jack Woltz, who found his thoroughbred horse's head in his bed, Harry Cohn.[1]

Las Vegas had survived multiple scandals and tough times.[2] The operation was extensive, and local and state politicians cooperated. Jewish Americans built most of the hotels.[3] Some of the early hotel names would survive, such as the Golden Nugget. Others, like the Apache, Pioneer Club, and Last Frontier would disappear into history. Reno had begun to fulfill its role as a mini-Las Vegas. Harrah's Reno advertised headliner singer Bobby Darin and comedian Larry Storch during Mickey's first month of freedom.

Mickey had minimal juice in the big Vegas loop. That didn't stop him from using his influence to catch up. He still ran most of the gambling in Los Angeles, and kept his nefarious influence at the Santa

Anita and Del Mar racetracks. There was still a little boxing action at the Hollywood Legion Stadium, between Vine and Gower. True to form, he resumed his regular role, in the company of beautiful actresses, and appeared down front at the local bouts, now considered secondary to venues like Las Vegas. His dates were impressed when Frank Sinatra stopped by to kiss his friend "Michael" on the cheek. Other times it was Sammy Davis or Redd Foxx who dazzled Mickey's escorts.

On January 25, 1972, Mickey, accompanied by his associate Jim Smith, visited his parole officer at the U.S. Courthouse in Los Angeles.

"I don't want nothing—no notoriety, no publicity," Mickey told reporters waiting for him at the courthouse.

Deputy U.S. Probation Officer Stuart Makagon told him to return once a month, and explained that the parole supervision would last five years—the remainder of his term.

Despite all his contrite speeches, Mickey pursued his old line of work, being the boss, now somewhat of a pretense. He sent messages around the country, trying to rekindle his old relationships. They read, "Tell —— I said hello, if you ever see him around." He would tell anyone within earshot that he lived on loans and couldn't afford a car. The size of his operation had diminished, but that didn't stop him from living well: the skim arrangements with the slick organized national network provided immediate cash flow. Reliable friends keep him living in luxury; Frank Sinatra supplied a quick $25,000, and a promise of more. Not everyone was happy to see Mickey out of prison. Joe DiCarlo, who was now making tons of money as Sonny and Cher's manager, never paid him back any of the money he had shelled out for legal fees during the Whalen matter.

The IRS still watched Mickey, and forced him to live without reporting any income—not that he suddenly had decided to become a law-abiding taxpayer. If he did, they would collect a chunk of it. He found it impossible to get a court order to collect the money that attorney Belli had won for him from the government, the only known bulk income possibility.

"Criminally rehabilitated" Mickey moved to a smallish apartment at 1014 Westgate in West Los Angeles. Times had changed, and many places initially refused the celebrity tenant's request for occupancy.

After eleven years in prison, he naturally found the adjustment to civilian life a slow process. He arranged physical therapy appointments at UCLA Medical Center through a Dr. Rubenstein, where he complained about the high cost of health care.[4]

Despite his ordeal, he never sounded bitter. He was more interested in reporting on his exploits than on how it had affected him, but remained critical of prison conditions. It was hard for him to accept that the society he loved—and loved to pillage—could take such a subhuman approach to prisoners. He continued to seek the limelight, and made a public case for prison reform.

Mickey traveled around the country talking to the old crowd, and lectured his fans. He visited with Owney Madden's widow Agnes in Hot Springs, Arkansas; Carlos Marcello in New Orleans; the remaining Cleveland mob; and those who had flocked to Vegas.

Separating himself from his origins, he adopted the stance that the crime world was full of Young Turks and "freaks," the latter a new breed of criminal that didn't share his mixed morality. The old rules were gone.

The bad-guy-turned-good-guy told reporters, "That's the whole problem, nobody has any shame, or respect, or pride anymore." Mickey lamented the days when a handshake sealed the deal, when friendship and a man's word meant everything.

He keenly observed the change in business: "Today, well, you couldn't even trust a signed contract—if you had one."

He admonished the past and told all reporters that he did not intend to resume his decadent life, repeating often, "I've had my belly full of it." He denied any illicit activity. "I live like I lived before, but I'm not into what you would call any action. I don't know if I'm living on my reputation or what, but very seldom can I go to any kind of affair where I'm not asked for my autograph."

Mickey-the-celebrity appeared on the Merv Griffin television variety show in 1972, his first year out of prison. Prime-time Mickey made the most of his spot, and offered his trademark statement that he never killed a man who didn't deserve it.

His fan mail rivaled that of any movie star. Some of the letters asked for his help, but a few wanted to give him gifts. Strangers offered him houses in Glasgow (Scotland), Florida, and Wyoming. A letter in French asked if he was interested in a gambling business near the Alps.

On January 16, 1973, Mickey lost his brother. Seventy-year-old Harry Marvin Cohen was the victim of a hit-and-run driver. He was in front of his Oxford Avenue home at seven in the evening when a foreign car, possibly a Renault, struck him. A second car traveling in the opposite direction also struck him. The first driver sped away. Police did not hold the second driver, only sixteen-years-old. Harry died at Hollywood Presbyterian Hospital. The police all-points bulletin for a black foreign car with a white top did not provide any leads.

On March 9 longtime Mickey pal Eli Lubin died of a heart attack at age fifty-two. Lubin was in the furniture business, but his obit naturally mentioned his Mickey associations, particularly the

Pearson beating, and his own $10,000 tax evasion fine.

Four days later, Mickey opened a restaurant called Sonny's on La Cienega Boulevard, the fashionable restaurant row area of eastern Beverly Hills. Another Mickey acquisition was Paoli's in San Francisco, his steak and occasional cash source while he was in prison. He had hopes of opening another Paoli's at the Century Plaza Hotel, the favorite of Ronald Reagan and George Bush. He also made plans to open a restaurant in Beverly Hills called La Famiglia, which would become home to many Rat Packers, including nightly regular Dean Martin.[5] He also opened Gatsby's in Brentwood, not far from his apartment. The FBI was certain that Gatsby's was a front for gambling. By the end of 1973, he was back to bookmaking, business as usual.

Mickey spent his nights at popular Chasen's, Scandia, Gatsby's, Perino's, Matteo's, the Playboy Club, and in bars

like the West Side Room. He liked to have
a drink in the evening, although he didn't
want his public to think that he ever
imbibed.

One of the most popular Beverly Hills
hangouts was the Luau restaurant,
complete with indoor lagoon, celebrities,
and high-priced hookers. He avoided it,
despite its action-every-night reputation,
because Lana's former husband Steve
Crane owned it. Mickey did not want to
relive the Turner-Stompanato episode or
the old revenge accusations by her.

His name was on the publicity sheets for
premieres and new clubs. He was proud of
his opening night tickets for venues like
the modern Shubert Theater in newly
constructed Century City, adjacent to
Beverly Hills, and built on the old 20th
Century Fox back lot.

The Italian mob, whose pejorative
nickname the "Mickey Mouse Mafia"
seemed to fit more over time, didn't
improve its chances for dominance when

Dominic Brooklier took over in 1974. He is most remembered for ordering a hit on "The Bomp."

Long-time Mickey and Nixon pal Murray Chotiner died under suspicious circumstances that fueled conspiracy theories related to Henry Kissinger and General Al Haig. On January 23, 1974, Chotiner was in an automobile accident with a government truck in McLean, Virginia. Rumors suggested that the driver of the truck was a naval officer. First reports indicated that he had suffered only a broken leg; he died a week later in a hospital. Some relate his death to a decision by Kissinger to have General Haig issue a report on President Nixon's organized crime connections, which included Chotiner's shady history. Kissinger and Haig hoped that Nixon would resign. Chotiner's widow had no legal recourse since President Gerald Ford had pardoned Nixon.

The L.A. Press Club invited Mickey to speak in 1974. He sat at the dais next to associate Jim Smith. He kept a box of tissues within reach: his OCD never dissipated; he had his housekeeper alcohol everything in his home. Even after she cleaned the bathroom, Mickey felt it was necessary to give the sink the once over before using it.

For multiple reasons, including his own personality traits of self-doubt and low self-esteem, Mickey was still disappointed in himself. He lamented, "I was just a plain vulgar heist man. I hadn't been around with a lot of good decent people... Even right now, I'm not too sure of myself, although I have gained some confidence."

He craved the type of fame and universal acceptance that surrounded the Rat Pack. The lengthy prison sentence didn't help his reputation. He was unable to achieve the social status afforded most celebrities, and could not mingle in all elements of society. Even though he had become a celebrity in his own right, he knew that he was not welcome in certain social, political, and business circles. Mickey despised performing what he called "dirty work" for many prized citizens because hours later the same people would ignore him in public. Yet, one of the country's most prominent citizens would soon call upon him for help.

6.

Fate thrust Mickey back into the national spotlight. The anti-capitalist Symbionese Liberation Army kidnapped Patricia Hearst from her Berkeley apartment on February 4, 1974. She subsequently appeared in a videotape robbing a bank with her kidnappers. Her father Randolph Hearst contacted Mickey. Likely Ed Montgomery, a crime reporter for the *San Francisco Examiner,* suggested the aging bookie since he was an old Hearst family friend and someone well versed in the criminal arts. Mickey "begrudgingly" agreed to assist, out of respect for Randolph's father

William Randolph, who had always befriended Mickey and had regularly suggested that he enter legitimate business.

He seized the opportunity to act the role of the elder statesman and dealmaker, a matured stance he thoroughly enjoyed, and looked forward to the public lapping up his participation. As Ben Hecht once predicted of criminals, "And he will become as full of nonsense as a Secretary of State." Mickey had aged and slipped graciously "into the tame ways of the voting population." In a videotaped interview in which he spoke about the Hearsts, he looked haggard but well fed. He appeared in a neat short-sleeved sport shirt, and by this time he looked like everyone's Jewish grandfather from Encino, with thinning hair and whitish bushy eyebrows.

When the Hearsts first planned their visit with Mickey, the most difficult element of the arrangements involved the

restaurant selection. The Hearsts
naturally wanted to go to popular
Chasen's, home of movie stars, high-
ranking politicians, and the moneyed
crowd. It was closed every Monday, the
day of the meeting. They mentioned their
other preferences, Scandia and Matteo's,[1]
but those were also closed. The Hearsts
finally settled on Gatsby's for the Monday,
October 7 meeting. They flew in from
Hillsborough after Hearst attorney James
M. MacInnis finalized the details.

Mickey said of the legal counsel, "I know
Jim very well, and have for some
time...he's been a visitor in my home and
I see him whenever I go to San Francisco."

Thirty-six-year-old Jim Smith picked up
the Hearsts and MacInnis at Los Angeles
International Airport around six-thirty. He
told reporters, "I drove them to the
restaurant for dinner... But I didn't take
part in the conversation. That was
between them and Mickey."

Gatsby's "owner" Bill Rosen warned Mickey that the local police intelligence squad was at the restaurant before the Hearsts arrived.

Mickey recalled that after a few drinks, Patty's mother Catherine Hearst revealed that they didn't think rescuing Patty from her kidnappers was prudent because she would face a prison term immediately upon her return. He was disappointed with the present understanding between the Hearsts and the authorities. He was surprised that the Hearsts hadn't negotiated a better arrangement before bringing him into the loop. He didn't like the deal, accustomed as he was to brokering deals that were clear between all parties, often well in advance. He refused to locate anyone that might serve twenty or thirty years in prison.

Mickey described his dismay: "When I learned that, it was a shock to me because I thought they knew what they were doin'. When I learned that they didn't have it in that kind of a shape I says, 'lookit, I won't bring nobody in to go to prison.'"

He watched as "Randy" Hearst and his attorney tried to chastise Catherine for misrepresenting the legal aspects of the dilemma.

Smith told reporters that after a two-hour meeting he drove the Hearsts and their attorney back to the airport around ten-thirty.

At the airport, the FBI watched as local police stopped them, MacInnis, and Mickey. Two detectives ordered the three men to put their hands up against the wall. One detective asked Catherine Hearst for identification. When she was unable to produce any proper documents the eager detective said, "We'll have to place you under arrest for consorting with a known criminal."

Moments later the other detective calmed the overzealous one when all the authorities realized whom the police had rousted.

Mickey was clearly upset and did his best to apologize to the Hearsts "for the hassle."

It was more likely that he had actually heard about the long prison term facing Patty Hearst while at the airport, but he preferred to erase the airport incident from his memory. However, he did mention that "the intelligence squad" had stopped the Hearsts.

Mickey did express his concerns for Patty soon after the roust at the airport. "Hell, all this time I thought it was all fixed up—that the kid wouldn't have to go to jail... I've been there—I can't walk, only shuffle like a duck 'cause I was there."

The FBI had monitored the entire meeting, but refused to comment. Assistant Director William A. Sullivan from Los Angeles said that they were in close contact with the Hearsts.

Hearst did not deny the meeting. "It was no big deal... I'd rather not discuss it, frankly, but we did have dinner and we did talk about the situation... Mr. Cohen thought maybe he could be of some help, and he offered to do what he could. We don't know if we can help or not, but we thought it worthwhile to talk to him... He didn't ask for anything, certainly not for himself... He was trying to help and I don't want to say anything that would cause a problem." His rationale for contacting Mickey had more to do with Mickey's reputation in the black underworld.

"I was involved in gambling in other days in the black community. I have a lot of friends there that love me and that I love dearly," said Mickey.

He told *Los Angeles Times* reporter Bill Hazlett, "I offered to help in any way I could, and I've already laid out some of my own money—not much, $250 here, $300 there—for some meetings and a couple of plane tickets."

The dapper Sherlock Holmes made the most of the expanded publicity routes and appeared on Los Angeles television

Thursday night, October 24, to discuss the entire Hearst saga.

Mickey had tried to contact SLA leader Donald DeFreeze after multiple meetings with others. (DeFreeze was killed soon thereafter.) He was able to reach three people who were either SLA members or close associates; one was in Soledad Prison. Reporter Ed Montgomery had suggested that Mickey try the prison. He ended up with two solid leads, supplied by a white woman and a black man known to a numbers operator. Some reports suggested that Mickey met with Emily and Bill Harris, also wanted by the FBI. He refused to reveal the location of the meeting. The nature of his rendezvous surprised him. "You know, it was really sort of weird—like one of those cloak and dagger things you see on TV. Go here, then go there..."

Mickey said in many interviews, "You know. I speak their language. The cops don't-—the FBI don't. But I do. So it took a little time. But finally I got a lead that was good."

By October 25, rumors had cropped up that he had located Patty Hearst in a city near the U.S.-Canadian border. He immediately denied the story. "I have never seen Patricia Hearst and I have never talked to her. The information I got about her came second, third, fourth, and fifth hand." The new facts had originated with San Francisco television reporter Marilyn Baker, and then became a widely disseminated UPI story.

Reporters checked with Catherine Hearst, who told them, "Mr. Cohen offered to use his underworld connections in an effort to find Patty. He never told us he had seen her and he didn't say anything about her being in one town or another or anything about the Canadian border." Catherine Hearst was critical of reporter Marilyn Baker, whom Catherine felt was fueling the story to "...keep herself in the public eye."

Based on what Mickey represented as a clairvoyant hunch, he somehow pinpointed Patty Hearst's previously unknown location as Cleveland; more likely, Montgomery had directed Mickey there and then rescinded the suggestion. The current speculation on Patty's whereabouts included the West Coast, Canada, Panama, and Guatemala.

The day after the Baker-UPI story broke, Mickey washed his hands of the whole matter: "I've done the best I could, but it just didn't work out... I thought I could help and I hoped to be successful in getting her back... I didn't—I failed, and it's all over."

Mickey actually had had all the details in place before his October 7 meeting with the Hearsts. He initially had flown in several of his Cleveland contacts for advice. Once he had planted the word, he waited for the results to materialize. He explained the plan: "I was supposed to

have gone to Cleveland myself if arrangements could have been made to speak to
Patty Hearst and relay to her a message
from her parents: all her parents were
interested in was her well-being and
safety. If she would come back and clear
herself of all these charges, and if they
were assured of her welfare, then if she
chose to go back to the radical way of life
and—to use the words of the Hearsts—'to
live a life like Jane Fonda,' it would be OK
with them."

When the SLA threatened a shootout,
Mickey backed off on pressuring a meeting
with Patty. "I'm on parole, and that's all I
needed for a goddamned shootout to
happen and somebody getting killed," he
said. Furthermore, consorting with the
wrong people was enough to raise a parole
officer's eyebrows.

He explained, "I couldn't go where she
was at. The people I got involved with,
they thought I was going to where she was
at." Mickey told the *New York Times* that

if he could have traveled to Cleveland, he would have delivered Patty back unharmed.

He said, "...that I would have to use force to bring her in." The feisty sleuth also admitted that he was afraid for his own safety: "...a little scared to talk with them SLA members... Hell, they're wild kids, those kinds. You know, jittery, shaky. You don't ever know what they're going to do."

To make matters worse, Patty wasn't ready to leave the SLA, and nothing Mickey or anyone else could do would influence that decision.

Randolph Hearst, rightly fearful of harm coming to his daughter, told reporters that it was unlikely that Mickey had located her. The Hearsts always maintained that they had rejected Mickey's offer. MacInnis, attorney for the Hearsts, later confirmed to reporters that Mickey did locate Patty in Cleveland through black radicals and people connected to the numbers racket.

He said, "It was a definite thing, and it was a definite thing she was coming back to San Francisco."

Gentleman Mickey uttered his original final word on the juxtaposed stories and politicking: "I don't want to be rude, but I got to beg off this thing."

Mickey's elder statesman adventures would continue, again putting him in the spotlight.

7.

News regarding the original possibility of
Mickey's presidential pardon hit the
papers again on October 27, 1972. Jack
Anderson, who took over for Drew Pearson
at the *Washington Post*, said that the
pardon angle from President Johnson had
been possible. He explained that Pearson
had visited Mickey in prison several times.
Pearson, who spoke often with Mickey,
also had President Johnson's ear, and
Anderson concluded that a compassionate
friend like Pearson could easily have asked
Johnson about a pardon for Mickey.

Mickey's voice displayed his anger and
disappointment whenever he spoke about

Johnson. "Drew Pearson had it right when he wrote about it. Johnson promised me a full medical pardon through Pearson. Pearson was a friend of mine. He visited me in jail regularly."

He said that Pearson wrote this memo to him: "I got a definite promise from LBJ that one way or another, if Humphrey wins or loses, you're going to get a parole or a medical parole at least."

Many articles contained his laments regarding the pardon. "I know he [Drew Pearson] didn't lie to me. I was to get that pardon after the 1968 campaign no matter what. Everybody thought Humphrey would win. But I was to get that pardon... So sure, I was involved in the 1968 race between Nixon and Humphrey. But how can you do much from the pen? ... So what happens? Nixon beats Humphrey, and that S.O.B. Johnson died... [As did Drew, of course. And Mickey's still in jail until they give him a parole]. I should have had that pardon." (Johnson died the year after Mickey left prison.)

With Pearson and LBJ gone, there was little chance to prove the promise, not that either party would have jumped at the opportunity. Anderson had none of secretive Pearson's files, so it was impossible to check his letters.

Mickey felt strongly that all the politicians had double-crossed him. He was also quick to speak to the media concerning his dealings with Murray Chotiner and Nixon, and the story circulated once again.

Word was out that Mickey was writing a book about his life. John Peer Nugent had received a $7,500 advance to start work on the autobiography. Mickey told reporters on October 26, "I tell it all...all that I know...like it was." Mickey wasn't sure if the book would be published. "These lawyers are worried about lawsuits and statutes of limitation and things like that. I'm not. It's the truth—and that's more than I can say for some of those books everybody reads."

On November 13, 1974, John Hall elaborated in the *Los Angeles Times* about his evening out with Mickey at Gatsby's. Journalist Hall still found him a man with flare. Mickey enjoyed his veal plate while he reminisced about his youth, his prison stay record, his speech and writing tutor from twenty years ago, his dislike for Muhammad Ali—"Cassius Clay is a rotten example for kids"—and his upcoming biography. He liked fighter Bobby Chacon, but said that he had quit and didn't give it his all against Ruben Olivares.

Balding Mickey kept his cane nearby, complained about his legs, and popped antacids for an ulcer. He dressed in a "neat, conservative, expensive" suit with a perfectly knotted tie. Waiters watched his every move, tried to anticipate his needs, and could not do enough for him. He handed out tips to the waiter, cocktail girl, maître d', and busboy. He washed his hands with lemon water, and dried them with a large white napkin.

He made it clear that he lived on loans and had no money for luxury items. His book was in limbo until the IRS agreed on profit-sharing terms. He said that he did collect the government award for his Atlanta prison experience, this time adding that the money went to the IRS. He excused himself from dinner to check a tape of his recent talk show interview.

Mickey continued his regular publicity campaign, and during the first week of March 1975, his extensive AP interview with Linda Deutsch circled the globe. He was looking forward to the end of his parole in eighteen months and explained how his life had changed: "I live practically the same life I lived before. The only difference is that I'm not involved with gambling or any illegal activities... Not that I've lost all my friends or contacts... Everyone comes to see me. And I'm out to all my old haunts... I just don't have the strength or stomach to get involved in anything."

He spent part of each day doing his physical therapy exercises. He enjoyed going to the movies, and remarked that both *Godfather* movies were accurate depictions of mob life.

He made sure to plug his book, which was still in the works. "A lot of my friends are prejudiced. They think this is gonna be bigger than the *Godfather*. I really wrote the truth."

The new author spoke about his disappointment with the Hearsts: "It was a heartrending thing anyway. My sisters kept bothering me about it."

He said that Al Capone was one of his favorite people, explaining that he only showed love and respect, although Mickey commented that he had never seen Capone angry.

Mickey had become critical of Las Vegas:

I remember when there were only two roads to Vegas. It was a little frontier town. My place was the first one in town... The environment is so different now. The color seems to be lacking... It's become an assembly line. They used to cater to a more gambling element. Now you see women and children running up to the slot machines... It takes a lot of glamour out of gambling.

The fastidious dandy still tried to cut a dapper image, and was meticulous about his clothing. His social life hadn't diminished, and he dated actress Lita Baron, who was divorced from actor Rory Calhoun. He also spoke fondly of Gail Fisher, who worked on the hit television series *Mannix*.

Mickey lamented about his physical difficulties. "...if I never came out of that coma I just wouldn't have known what hit me. Sometimes walking is so painful... There were times when I could do things with a snap of my finger. It's not quite like that anymore."

He also looked on the bright side: "...it's good to be with a pretty girl or with company I enjoy, at a prizefight or a restaurant I enjoy."

The criminal pundit was rarely out of the media spotlight. Newspapers published his speculations on the disappearance of Jimmy Hoffa through July of that year. He called the Hoffa matter a "setup"; the whole Hoffa meeting was a ruse.

Mickey spoke with reporter Bill Hazlett. "I think Jim fell into a trap that somebody set for him because of an internal squabble in the union... I've got my own ideas about that but I certainly can't talk about that on the telephone."

He begged off on giving the information to the Hoffa family. "I didn't want to take away any of the hopes that Jimmy, Jr., Barbara, or his wife, Josephine, might have. It just wouldn't be right."

During August, he still spoke to reporters about Hoffa. He explained that people in Detroit had asked him to use his contacts to help locate Hoffa. He said, "I'm trying in every way to find out what the score is." A few more Hoffa and Mickey stories circulated around the country. He finally said by telephone: "I feel Jim is gone... I know what I know from my own connections." He was correct regarding Hoffa's execution.

Whenever possible, he appeared on television. On Friday, September 19, 1975, Mickey joined former attorney general and political activist Ramsey Clark (currently Saddam Hussein's attorney) on a ninety-minute show, part of the Wide World of Entertainment, entitled "The Underworld: A Portrait in Power." Actor Robert Stack hosted the television show, and the two guests discussed "the power of organized crime."

Just ten days later, Mickey entered UCLA Medical Center for a suspected abdominal tumor, and doctors performed immediate exploratory surgery.

On October 1, doctors removed most of his stomach at UCLA. He had been suffering from cancer, not simply an ulcer, although doctors referred to his tumor as a malignant ulcer. Dr. Herbert Machleder presided over a team of surgeons during the three-hour procedure.

Old companion Liz Renay visited Mickey the day before and the day after his operation. She told reporters, "He told me that he had cancer and was on the way out. He said he knew it was a down approach to take, but that he knew he was dying."

She offered Mickey's long-standing quote, but changed it to read that he had killed "no one who didn't deserve it."

Two days later doctors offered a good prognosis for Mickey, and his condition was now listed as satisfactory.

He "wrote" his book, complete with the misspelled names of his legal associates, employees, acquaintances, and even his barber "Gelbar[t]." Naturally, the movie buzz was back in Mickey's life.

He wanted to set the record straight, and clear up misrepresentations by critical author Ed Reid, and others. Yet, his book did little to outline a linear history, or shed light on unsettled events. He was still in denial about his past, which accounts for some of his omissions. Many people also had high stakes in what he was willing to spill in his book. His rambling dialogue supplied the censorship, edited from years of retelling the stories. Diplomat Mickey was not looking for any more trouble; he was more interested in cultivating his image as one of the first talking head pundits.

Even his unique autobiography, one of the few memoirs having to do with organized crime, has become the subject of a cover-up since it appears censored. He was one of the stronger links between the unholy alliance of the entertainment business and organized crime, a relationship he cherished. Since some of the rich and powerful allowed Mickey into their lives, he was in a position of great influence and, as mentioned, often resorted to blackmail in order to solidify his control of celebrities. He wasn't talking, despite knowing where many of the Hollywood skeletons were buried, and does not give up much in his book, certainly none of the salacious celebrity stories that people crave. His mixed morality and revisionist view of his life prevented him from revealing the backroom politics either.

Author Michael Collins Piper suggests that John Peer Nugent, the writer who penned the autobiography from Mickey's long-winded stories, was subject to CIA editing: "Interesting enough, Nugent himself once participated in a debate with JFK assassination investigator, A. J. Weberman, co-author of *Coup d'Etat in America*, where he—Nugent—sought to refute CIA complicity in the assassination."[1]

By the time his autobiography hit the shelves during late 1975, the country was still in the midst of severe a cocaine epidemic. The illicit coffers overflowed with the success of the international drug trade. The white powder was everywhere, a staple to many in the entertainment business, as it was on the set of the new late night television comedy hit *Saturday Night Live*.[2]

Resilient Mickey didn't give in easily to the cancer. The old boxer walked with a limp, his right leg almost useless. By the end of November 1975, he was on his feet and in Manhattan to promote his book. He sat for interviews in his elegant suite at the Pierre Hotel, across from Central Park. One interview was with journalist Ira Berkow. Mickey, wisely not trusting the cleanliness of hotel housekeeping, sat on a clean white bed sheet, draped over a chair. Berkow noted the star sapphire pinkie ring, platinum watch, and half-dollar sized golf cuff links, all on loan or gifts from friends. He wore a three-piece glen-plaid suit that fit nicely on his "solid frame."

Mickey reflected on his past, surrounded by oak walls and Degas reproductions. "He [Nixon] was a big help to me in my operations in Orange County...but if you ever told me that he'd be president I would have died laughing."

The showman went down memory lane, and spoke about Al Capone, who would always "lay a couple of hundred dollar bills in my pocket."

Regarding Mickey's murder record, he admitted to six, "but every one of 'em needed killing."

Frank Sinatra was "A stand-up guy, and if you call his hole card, he's going to answer."[3]

The crime philosopher added that Jimmy Hoffa was buried in a lime pit, and that should serve as a deterrent to the youth of America who pursue criminal careers.

Berkow sensed the frailty of the elder criminal: "...one looked at him and his tissues and wondered if in some subconsciously humanitarian way, he was, in the end, not so much fearful of being contaminated as he was concerned with contaminating."

In another interview, Mickey told *New York News* writer Anthony Burton that the assassination attempts on his life numbered twelve. He again spoke of his love for Al Capone.

He lamented the bombing death of an old Cleveland associate Alex "Shondor" Birns. He found out about the death after a reporter had mailed him the press clippings. To show his gratitude, he sent the reporter a cashmere sweater.

Burton liked his subject. "That too, for Mickey Cohen, was class."

Toward Christmas 1975, UPI circulated a story about Mickey. The article spoke about his flamboyant life, how his world appeared modeled on the movie life of James Cagney, George Raft, and Edward G. Robinson. The story mentioned his lavish wardrobe, his association with strippers who wore fur coats and diamonds, how he hobnobbed with movie stars, and unfortunately his five-foot-three stature and elevator shoes.

The same year, producers released an offbeat documentary about the Kennedy assassinations entitled *I Due Kennedy* (The Two Kennedys). The piece, originally released in Italy in 1969, featured Mickey footage along with Fidel Castro, Ramsey Clark, Al Capone, Carlos Marcello, Hubert H. Humphrey, Barbara Hutton, Lyndon Johnson, Ted Kennedy, Phyllis McGuire, and Benito Mussolini. *The Two Kennedys* had all the voices dubbed except Lauren Bacall, Marilyn Monroe, and Hitler.

In summer 1976, the *compares* buried long-time mobster Johnny Rosselli in a fifty-five gallon oil drum, but not before sawing off his legs. After tossing the drum in the ocean, they renamed him Deep-Six Johnny.[4]

Mickey's book did not make a big splash. It never became the hit to bring him back to the forefront of Hollywood; he had been out of the limelight too long. Hollywood's memory was always a short one. The public had new idols; bad boys of rock took center stage and grabbed the headlines. The public relegated him to history, but he was as much a part of the nation's fixation with Hollywood as any matinee idol or actor turned politician.

On July 6, 1976, he returned to UCLA hospital, complaining of fatigue. Further diagnosis revealed that he was suffering from jaundice. He remained in the hospital until July 20.

Mickey died quietly in his sleep on Thursday, July 29, just weeks before the end of his parole. Some references cite a coronary as the cause of death, likely secondary to his deteriorating bout with cancer.

Ironically, he held the record for surviving unsuccessful murder attempts, and none of his adversaries ever dreamed he would still be around that year.

When he died, Mickey's net worth, including his cash, was $3,000. His will, filed for probate on August 5, indicated a twenty-five percent share for "right-hand-man" Jim Smith, and fifteen percent shares for Smith's children, James and Tina. Sisters Pauline Duitz and Lillian Weiner each received fifteen percent. The U.S. Attorney in Los Angeles was suing Mickey for back taxes totaling $496,535.23. The debt was over ten years old.

About 150 people attended Mickey's funeral. Only one shoving match started during the services; it involved a photographer. Funeral officials would not reveal the names of the guests at the private service.

Meyer Harris Cohen lies in a crypt at Hillside Cemetery in Culver City, final resting place of the stars. He would have been pleased with the view, an endless list of Hollywood luminaries and their monuments. His neighbors run the gamut from comedian Jack Benny to singer Dinah Shore and from Stooge Moe Howard to immortal makeup czar Max Factor.

He lies in the mausoleum's second drawer from the bottom, the Alcove of Love, A-217. The plaque reads, "Our Beloved Brother, Meyer H. Cohen, Mickey, 1914–1976."

Obits around the country quoted Mickey on his sense of ethics and repeated his trademark lines. Estimates on his mansion reverted to the quarter of a million-dollar range.

The *Los Angeles Times* obituary stated that he was "the undisputed boss of Los Angeles gangdom and lived in a mansion surrounded with an electronically equipped fence and spotlights and containing closets filled with expensive suits and shoes...traveled in a Cadillac followed by another car carrying his armed "helpers." The *New York Times* called him "the tough little former professional boxer who rose to become a leader of the West Coast gambling rackets in the 1950s and 1960s..."

Melvin Belli recalled Mickey less than two months after his death: "Mickey Cohen was a very sweet, gentle guy."

Actor Harvey Keitel, who played Mickey in the movie *Bugsy,* knew his character well. "A guy like that could have been anything in life—had he had the right guidance he could have gone anywhere in life because his drive, his intellect...it was all there."

Mickey's former wife LaVonne had experienced the multilayered personality firsthand: "...behind all the excitement and violence that surrounds his life is a guy who is very easy to like. There is nothing mean about Mickey. He is

166

generous and kind in his own way, but he would rather die than admit it."

Ben Hecht had once summarized Mickey's positive side:

> He paid off on the dot and to the nickel. He fixed fights and let his pals in on the take. He operated hideaway gambling rendezvous where the dice, wheels and cards were as on the level as any operator could afford to have them. On the side he beat up Nazi propagandists, staked bums to binges, never overlooked the birthday of a policeman's kid, paid medical bills for all wounded supporters and was good for a touch from anybody who smiled and said, "Hello, Mickey."

Crime historian James Johnston was likewise enamored but reminds us that "Mickey was one of the nicest killers you'd ever want to meet."

Peter Noyes recognized Mickey's influence: "Mickey Cohen was a big name in this town. You didn't get any bigger than the Mick." He was larger than life, larger than Hollywood life. He was the underdog who defied everyone in town, and became an international celebrity because of his criminal notoriety.

Life magazine wove him into the social fabric of the nation. "In the Rat Pack Era, the guys and dolls were having a time; Sinatra swingin', Vegas sizzlin', and one brazen gangster struttin' his stuff."

Hecht may have said it best: "The Republic's most colorful, and, for a long time, most successful criminal, Mr. Cohen."

That was Mickey.

Epilogue

For the next three decades, mobsters floated through the Sunset Strip and Beverly Hills oasis, while the commercial and social transition from Hollywood continued west.

The fashionable "Bomp" was one of the most visible Italian figures. In 1977, Chicago associate Tony Spilotro likely gave the orders to have The Bomp, who was blabbing extensively to the FBI, shot and killed. Four bullets in the head from a silenced automatic pistol felled the spiffy assassin. The local goomba Mickey Mouse Mafia continued to decline due to failed leadership.

The Two Tonys gruesome murder case would have remained unsolved, but Jimmy "The Weasel" Fratianno spilled this and more—he killed five times for Jack Dragna—when he had entered the Federal Witness Protection program two years after Mickey died.

Mickey's journalist friend seventy-eight-year-old Agnes Underwood sued Fratianno in 1981 over the false claim that she wrote the story about the fake ship destroyed on its way to deliver Israeli armaments, suggesting that she was in on the fundraising fraud. Fratianno's statements had resulted in years of published false accusations against Mickey. The $110,000,000 defamation suit stated that Underwood first heard about the much-bandied Fratianno quote from her grandson after television's *60 Minutes* ran the story. Underwood's attorney Caryl Warner insisted that no such *Herald-Express* article ever existed, and that Underwood didn't meet Mickey until 1948. Fratianno claimed that he *never made* the statement, and had no idea how his biographer Ovid Demaris got that idea. He said that it was Demaris' responsibility to fact check. Also named in the suit were Mike Wallace, still of *60 Minutes*, the *New York Times Book Co.*, radio station KMPC, and KMPC's Billy Rose.

Underwood said, "I never took 5 cents from anyone, and now they are accusing me of stealing a million."

CBS and KMPC refused to retract their statements.

In January 1982, *Playboy*'s Hugh Hefner ran into problems with Mickey's old pal Joe DiCarlo after helping him set up Pips, a fancy and exclusive private club in Los Angeles that featured backgammon. Hefner said he was aware of DiCarlo's past, but never considered it a problem, and had resigned from Pips over a control dispute. When Hefner sought a gaming license in New Jersey, authorities brought up Mickey's name.

Mickey's exquisite custom-built car ended up in the hands of Negri's Antique and Classics on Mt. Baldy Circle in Fountain Valley, California. Owner Frank Negri advertised the car for his 1982 Memorial Day Collector Car Auctions and Show, but it was not part of the auction; it went on display with *Waltons'* John Boy Model A Ford Coup and vehicles from the *CHiPS* police series. Negri explained: "The younger generation will probably not remember Mickey Cohen, but he was a colorful character...and we will have his bullet-proof Caddie at the show."

Through the eighties, the Los Angeles Strike Force identified brothers Peter and Carmen Milano, sons of Cleveland mobster Anthony Milano, as the local bosses. Informant brothers Craig and Lawrence Fiato wore FBI wires for six years right under the Milanos' noses. In May 1987, the last remnants of organized crime supposedly disappeared with the conviction of the Milano brothers. The eighteen-count indictment alleged, among other things, that they had plotted the murder of Louie Dragna (Jack's nephew) with Cleveland boss Jack Licavoli. Peter Milano received six years on federal racketeering statutes. Mike Rizzitello, the next in command, was sentenced to thirty-three years for conspiracy to murder topless bar boss William Carroll. Carmen Milano received his sentence in July 2000. "I'm in the twilight years of my life, and I'll never be in this situation again," said disbarred attorney Milano. "I'm here to retire."

When the survivors of Mickey's organized clique went their separate ways, a new breed of independent, grandiose, and brazen criminals developed. Supposedly, and many wrote, when "Fat" Herbie Blitzstein was iced on January 6, 1997, it marked the end of any link to Mickey and the Mickey Mouse boys.[1]

The announcement echoed one from ten years before, when authorities had gotten the Milanos. Thirty years back, U.S. Deputy Attorney General Christopher had said that all crime around town was a local phenomenon. The FBI currently knew of at least 1,700 *made* mafia members.

Residents like to view potential crime as they do their movies, Hollywoodized—a more glamorous approach to white-collar crime and capers. Retired FBI agent William J. Rehder wrote, "Capers...are...crimes in which cunning and intelligence and careful planning trump weapons and violence...payoff is big, the methods stealthy, and nobody gets hurt... When a jewel thief in a tuxedo slips out of the masked ball and steals the duchess's diamond tiara from the safe hidden behind the cognac in the liquor cabinet, that's a caper..." Rehder knows the harsher reality as well as he does the Hollywood version: "...when an ex-con gang-banger puts a cap into a Beverly Hills jewelry store owner and does a smash-and-grab on the Rolexes under the glass counter, that's not a caper."

With the exception of Larry Flynt's Hustler club in Beverly Hills, Tiffany, Wolfgang Puck, The Gap, and banks have replaced the gambling joints, nightclubs, and movie theaters. Comedy clubs, dance clubs, and upscale restaurants and shops fill the Sunset Strip.

Crime goes on, but in ways that would be unfamiliar to Mickey. A local business, Beverly Hills Estates Funding, recently pulled off a $140,000,000 mortgage swindle. In the process, the investment firm Lehman Brothers took a hit for $60,000,000 in bad loans. Two Beverly Hills residents utilized the Internet for manipulating stock prices by posting false information on message boards. One local received a six-year sentence and had to pay $6,000,000 in restitution for a more complex money laundering conspiracy. He had operated for ten years, manipulating over thirty different stocks. The press release read, "...Beverly Hills businessman, real estate investor, and film producer, sentenced to six years in prison for money laundering and securities fraud." After a three-year investigation, the FBI nailed a dentist for health care fraud. Can you believe that she audaciously bilked insurance carriers by submitting false claims? A bogus Beverly Hills modeling school paid $50,000 in fines. Did you hear the one about the illegal prescription-writing doctor who sold millions in narcotics?

Despite the availability of computers and the worldwide Internet, criminals continued to make money the old-fashioned way, with the oldest profession. The LAPD announced the culmination of a two-year investigation dubbed "Operation White Lace." One of the largest prostitution rings in the history of Los Angeles and Beverly Hills was the focus of indictments issued in December 2002. Some of the fanciest hotels supplied the backdrop for escorts to make the most of their efforts. To save time, the Organized Crime Division of the district attorney's office should have checked the Beverly Hills yellow pages that had advertised Exclusive Girls Escort, European Blondes, and European Delight Escorts—the ones used by the targeted group—or the current Bad Girls, Fun Girls, and Playmates, with "Naughty" and "Escorts" in oversized type.

In January 2003, the Beverly Hills police answered a call from the famous Osbournes, who reported that an ICM agent had robbed them! The Osbournes had conducted a raffle that included a necklace worth fifteen grand. The agent won the raffle but the forever-play-by-the-rules first family of reality television claimed that the winner had to be an invited guest, and the ICM agent had been a party crasher.

The United States District Court grand jury filed a 110-count sixty-page federal racketeering indictment against sleuth-to-the-stars Anthony Pellicano. The February 2006 indictment sounds like a carbon copy of Mickey's extortion and wiretapping operation. The suit alleges that Pellicano used confidential police and law enforcement records, including the National Crime Information Center, to access information on actors Sylvester Stallone, Garry Shandling, Kevin Nealon, and Keith Carradine; journalists Anita Busch and Bernard Weintraub; powerhouse agents Bryan Lourd and Kevin Huvane; and former professional tennis player Lisa Bonder Kerkorian, who was married to three-times-her-age billionaire entertainment mogul Kirk Kerkorian. The wiretapping scheme, efforts to dig up dirt of any kind—"responsible for securing clients who were willing and able to pay large sums for the purpose of obtaining personal information of a confidential, embarrassing, or incriminating nature"— included an LAPD officer, phone company employees, and Pellicano's own software bugging engineer. The *New York Times* indicated that the "noir clichés" of Mickey's world survive: "...the scandal's tentacles have extended beyond show-business figures to reach people prominent in the rarefied worlds of fine art and classical music." Witnesses included hedge-fund manager and art collector Adam D. Sender, who needed Pellicano's services regarding a sour movie deal with producer Aaron Russo, and Jacqueline A. Colburn, the former ninth wife of arts patron Richard D. Colburn; she used Pellicano to wiretap her husband. Lawyer and art collector Alan S. Hergott had pointed Sender to entertainment lawyer Bert Fields (his wife is art consultant Barbara Guggenheim), who had suggested Pellicano.

Crime is here to stay, organized or not. *Zai nisht narish*—"Don't be a fool."

Chapter Notes

1. "I just got back from the conspiracy convention. Have you been? It's fun. Seven hundred conspiracy theorists all in one hotel, with the little name tags, 'Hello, my name is—none of your fucking business!'... In the lobby, I saw five people get off the elevator—what, you think thats a coincidence?"—Paul Krassner. "Little money can be had writing Marilyn Monroe was not killed by either or both the Kennedys"—Konstantin Sidorenko. "The only casualty is truth"—Gerald Posner. Some question the agenda of Posner's one-sided work, while others accept his professional rehabilitation of the Warren Commission Report.

1. JFK was the first president to sell major arms to Israel. "...architect of today's strong military alliance between Israel and the America"—Warren Bass. Eric J. Greenberg's review in the *Jewish Week* of Bass' recent book, *Support Any Friend: Kennedy's Middle East and the Making of the U.S.-Israel Alliance,* examines Kennedy's failed efforts to bring Egyptian President Nasser to the negotiating table. JFK conflicted with Israeli Prime Minister David Ben-Gurion over the future of Israel's nuclear weapons. Kennedy suspected that the Dimona facility was strictly for nuclear weapons development. He threatened the peace process, but was able to reach an unhappy compromise with new Prime Minister Levi Eshkol. Palestinian newspapers wrote that the JFK assassination was a Zionist conspiracy and Oswald, Ruby, and even Lyndon Johnson were all working for the Jews. "Such squalid surmise—four decades before Gallup polls would reveal that millions of Arabs blamed the Mossad for [9/11]—remains a sobering reflection on the

depths and distortions of anti-Israel animus in the Arab world"—Bass.

[2]. Nixon gave up via a televised statement at 3:10 a.m. from the Ambassador Hotel in Los Angeles. His wife Pat did not want him to concede. Sinatra had tried to call Nixon to urge him to give up, but the telephone operator at the hotel refused to put his call through. Nixon was no philo-Semite, but was ultimately pragmatic when it came to world politics concerning Israel.

[3]. The RFK-Monroe romance has become an accepted fact, appearing in the works of several reputable authors, including Anthony Summers, Seymour Hersh, and C. David Heymann. The authors rely on a variety of sources, including Hollywood detective Fred Otash, who had Peter Lawford's home wiretapped. The authors also cite an eyewitness, Jeanne Carmen, purported Monroe friend and neighbor. Sinatra employee and Marilyn confidant George Jacobs could never accept the fact that she had had sex with RFK, whom Jacobs called a "weasel."

[4]. Exner was born Judith Katherine Inmoor in 1934 to a successful architect father and former Bonwit's model mother. She spent her early adult life married to actor Billy Campbell. She would fall in love with prodigy singer Tony Travis, a handsome, wealthy Beverly Hills resident. Tony, as mentioned, was Travis Kleefeld, the son of a successful builder, and Kleefeld introduced Exner to a life of champagne and caviar. Travis also introduced her to the "big boys" at the Racquet Club in Palm Springs and the Beverly Hills Tennis Club. Their breakup found her at Beverly Hills shrink Dr. Sherman, whom she would continue to consult periodically. Exner became no stranger to Jewish

business moguls on both coasts. She knew everyone of power in the mob, politics, and entertainment. She became a victim of FBI surveillance. "Campbell (Exner) did not know Giancana's real name. To her he was simply Sam Flood. Giancana once told Exner after she had complained of her difficulty securing a room at the Plaza Hotel in New York, 'Don't worry, when you get there, call Joe DiMaggio...he'll get you a room'"— Bill Adler. Sinatra introduced Desi Arnaz to Exner, and pimped her to Joe Fischetti and Jack Entratter. "Judy was a mob moll and the mistress of my brother-in-law, the president of the United States. In 1960, Judy, then twenty-three, an aspiring actress, became the consort of Jack Kennedy. What made Judy more than just another presidential girlfriend was the other company she kept, notably John "Don Giovanni" Rosselli and Salvatore Sam "Momo" Giancana, both members in good standing of organized crime, not to mention the Central Intelligence Agency. This is a lurid tale, and the more one probes it, the more lurid it becomes"— Peter Lawford. The Church Committee assigned Exner a lawyer from Sargent Shriver's law firm. Shriver was JFK's brother-in-law; his daughter is married to Governor Arnold Schwarzenegger of California. "The guy [Giancana] even proposed marriage but she turned him down and that's all she wrote. Sam ditched her. Kennedy got killed, the Feds were all over her, and she fell head first into the bottle... This was Judy Campbell's favorite bubble [Dom Perignon]. Do you realize that was only a dozen years ago? Seems like a million"—Johnny Rosselli. In 1999, Exner would die of breast cancer at age sixty-five. JFK had once given her a diamond and ruby broach, with thirty full-cut diamonds set in platinum. After the JFK assassination, Giancana and Sinatra ignored Campbell, including one conspicuous snubbing at the Key Club in Palm Springs.

5. On October 12, 1964, less than a year after JFK's assassination, Mary Pinchot Meyer, 43 years old, was mysteriously murdered on a towpath in Georgetown while going for a walk, sparking conspiracy theories.

6. Phyllis McGuire of the McGuire sisters dated both Giancana and comedian Dan Rowan. Giancana bugged Rowan's hotel room simultaneously with the CIA, who helped Giancana. He hired Arthur J. Balletti, who left all the equipment out on the bed during a lunch break, to the dismay of maids who phoned police. Giancana died in his basement—his head was full of twenty-two caliber bullets—while his home-cooked sausage and beans continued to fry nearby. He was shot once in the back of the head, and six times in the mouth.

7. JFK was instrumental to the production of the Sinatra movie *The Manchurian Candidate.* "That's the only way that the film ever got made. It took Frank going directly to Jack Kennedy"—Richard Condon. "I hope it pisses the shit of them [the Kennedys]"—Frank Sinatra. After the JFK assassination, the prophetic film became the center of attention. Producers yanked the movie from reruns, since it dealt with a programmed assassination. Condon discussed the brainwashing of Lee Harvey Oswald, while Truman Capote would later spout that RFK assassin Sirhan Sirhan was another Manchurian candidate. Sinatra always suspected that Oswald assassin Jack Ruby was programmable. When Sinatra's son was kidnapped eight days after the JFK assassination, the fabled crooner felt that the mob had sent him a message to remain silent about anything that could implicate the

mafia in the assassination and its aftermath. "Kennedy glamorized politics and embraced danger, and Hollywood responded in kind... *The Manchurian Candidate*, in a sense, is an anthology of Cold War concerns that materialized at the height of the Cuban missile crisis to startle audiences with a baroque tale of mind control, assassination and conspiracy"—J. Hoberman. "...that concentration of ecstasy and violence which is the dream life of the nation"— Norman Mailer.

[8]. Giancana received free personal Rat Pack performances in Chicago anytime he asked. Sinatra and Dean Martin never refused Giancana's requests for free gigs, sometimes lasting as long as ten days.

2.

[1]. While RFK was instrumental in putting Mickey back in prison, Kennedy, the FBI, and local authorities couldn't stop the role of organized crime in Las Vegas' gargantuan development. The Justice Department had quickly assigned eighty-six investigators to Las Vegas when RFK took over. The first year of activity would bring only two convictions amongst 135 prostitution arrests. RFK's bold ambitions did not frighten the national organization.

[2]. When the 9th Circuit Court of Appeals rejected (two to one) attorney A. L. Wirin's request for bail on September 14, 1961, he vowed to take the case to the U.S. Supreme Court. Justice William O. Douglas was sympathetic, although cautious, since the United States District Court in Los Angeles and the United States Circuit Court in San Francisco had already said "no" to bail the first time around during the appeals

process. Douglas instinctively felt that Mickey would not flee. The Justice Department announced a new indictment on September 16, including charges of concealing assets. On October 12, Justice Douglas granted Mickey his release on bail of $100,000. Mickey's sister and her husband had pledged their business as security, their only source of income, and had influenced the justice's bail decision. His mother had signed an affidavit pledging the trust deed on her home, and part of her equity in Carousel Ice Cream. The FBI had information that the bond company, run by old pal Abe Phillips, was actually Mickey's. A strip club owner, a Beverly Hills barber, and a restaurateur in San Francisco who owned Paoli, had supplied the rest of the bail money. Mickey cites Paoli as the major source for his release bond. The U.S. District Court in Los Angeles blocked his release. His attorneys, including Jack Dahlstrum, spent the entire day in court on October 16. Abe Phillips stood ready to deliver the bond papers to prison authorities. Judge Leon R. Yankwich had Mickey asked for additional money, and the Stuyvesant Insurance Co. in Newark supplied the new bond. Justice Douglas eventually convinced Judge Yankwich to side with him and not hardball U.S. Attorney Thomas R. Sheridan.

3. The show business house was the former home of poker operator Morrie Kasoff, and later a famous-ten blacklisted screenwriter named Robert Adrian Scott, whose wife wrote the *Lassie* television series.

4. Problems arose, and Mickey relied on attorney A. L. Wirin. Chief U.S. Judge Pierson M. Hall entered the Valley Hospital for a three-day examination. Wirin had needed Hall to certify the appeal bond. Judges William C. Mathes and Yankwich got cold feet when asked to

help, and insisted that U.S. Judge George Boldt, who had originally sentenced Mickey, was the only one who could certify the process, even though Boldt had told Judge William M. Byrne to permit Mickey's release, pending the Supreme Court's disposition. On a Friday, Wirin made a difficult long distance call to Mexico City to speak with vacationing Judge Boldt. Thirty minutes after the expensive telephone call the legal tumult had paid off and authorities released Mickey. "... The Supreme Court let Mickey Cohen go. You know why they gave him bail? Because he was going to go to the World Court if he didn't get it from them. And the Supreme Court didn't want him doing that. Because then the people of the United States would find out and say, 'What the hell's this World Court that is over the Supreme Court?'"—Drew Pearson.

3.

[1]. Many of the inmate leaders were competitive with Mickey since most of them had never achieved his status or celebrity. It was obviously jealousy—Mickey was rich and powerful on the outside. However, many prison employees were enamored with Mickey's celebrity, and he received extra special attention from those impressed with books sent by Billy Graham, visits by Graham's father-in-law Dr. L. Nelson Bell, and letters from Sammy Davis, Jr.

[2]. The Democrats and Pearson did not release Mickey's full statement. Nixon lost again, without the Democrats smearing him with Mickey's recent detailed information. After the loss in California, fundraisers held a Lincoln Day Dinner at the St. George Hotel in Brooklyn for the defeated Republican

warrior. The packed dais included Governor Nelson Rockefeller, U.S. Senator Jacob Javits, and Attorney General Louis Lefkowitz. Tickets were at a premium for the red carpet event. The Republican Party refused to give up on resilient Nixon.

3. Pearson made the original mob allegations on his radio program in 1956 and 1959—that Mickey had "collected money from the underworld" and gave it to Nixon. Pearson labeled attorney Murray Chotiner an organizer and front man for Nixon. Surprisingly, the Democrats did not release the new information that Mickey had supplied until 1968, when Pearson ran the story October 31 in his syndicated *Washington Post* column with even more evidence, one year before his own death.

4. Archaic Alcatraz finally relocated the remaining thirty-eight inmates and closed on March 21, 1963, after RFK gave the order.

5. During 1979, the government investigated Carlos Marcello and Sam Sciortino, a mobster from San Francisco, concerning the bribery of a federal judge and recordings of associates bragging about the mob's connection to the RFK assassination. Phillip Rizzuto, New Orleans operator and cousin to Sciortino, said, "Yeah, so we put him outa business," referring to RFK.

6. McDonald, from St. Stephen, South Carolina, was initially incarcerated for forgery, but later received ten years for assaulting a Leavenworth prisoner. He died in the early 1970s.

7. Flamboyant Melvin Belli was a multi-layered piece of work who drove a Rolls Royce and ultimately supported three homes, including one fancy Hollywood Hills home with a swimming pool. He was a popular television guest for many years, and was never

shy about seeking publicity for his cases. Reporters lost count of his many wives; one Shinto marriage in Japan escaped records. Belli, also a pal of actor Errol Flynn, died in 1996 at age eight-eight.

8. Marcello, Trafficante, and Hoffa all receive honorable mentions when it comes to JFK's assassination. Johnny Rosselli was hardly a fan, either. There was no love lost between the mob and the Kennedys. Estimates on the contract to kill JFK were as high as $750,000.

9. Degenerate Ruby, who loved to brag about his mob connections, was the fifth of eight children. Surprisingly, he tried to stay in shape, and was not a big drinker or smoker. His father was a poor carpenter, and Ruby ended up in the Jewish Home Finding Society of Chicago. Eventually committed, Ruby's mother Fanny would "ramble and shriek in Yiddish, crochet compulsively, demand that others serve her meals...hit them and had delusions about having sex with them (her children)"—Seth Kantor. Ruby was a defiant, depressed, and frequently truant child. Before moving on to his career running seedy clubs, he worked with future boxer Barney Ross. The two men met Al Capone in 1926 at the Kit Howard Gymnasium in Chicago, and Ruby started delivering packages for him, while running with street gangs. Ruby, who suffered multiple head injuries during his life, loved to stand on stage, and act as master of ceremonies. "Yet Ruby also could present an apparently normal and jovial side, that of a club owner ready to ensure his patrons had a good time. He went out of his way to encourage Dallas policemen to visit his clubs, giving them reduced rates and free drinks"—Gerald Posner. Police arrested Ruby nine times during a fourteen-year

run, for charges ranging from carrying concealed weapons to serving liquor after hours. "Ruby often resorted to violence with his employees, and lost the tip of his left index finger when one bit it off during a scuffle. He beat one of his musicians with brass knuckles, cracked another's head with a blackjack, knocked another's teeth out, and put the club's handyman in the hospital with a severe beating. To avoid paying the club's cigarette girl $50 in back wages, he threatened to throw her down the stairs until she relented... He was not above attacking people from behind, kicking men in the groin or face once he had them to the floor, or even striking women... He was often malicious, forcing beaten victims to crawl out of the club on hands and knees"—Posner. Jim Garrison, in painting his picture of a gay assassination cabal that included David Ferrie, Lee Harvey Oswald, and Clay Shaw, reminds us that Ruby was bisexual and frequented gay clubs. "...Jack Ruby, whose homosexuality is clearly established in almost forty instances in the Warren volumes... Oswald...was victimized by Ferrie in adolescence...(older men preying on teenage boys) included Jack Ruby..."—Lamar Waldron. In 1959, gunrunner Ruby made more than two trips to Cuba, arming Castro. "The smuggling of arms to Cuba was overseen by Norman "Roughhouse" Rothman, a burly associate of Miami's mob boss Santos Trafficante, who managed Trafficante's Sans Souci in Havana. At the same time Rothman reportedly was splitting Havana slot machines with Batista's brother-in-law... Ruby was part of the Rothman operation"—Jim Marrs. Rothman had signed the rental agreements for the airplanes that transported the guns. He also had an interest in the Biltmore Terrace Hotel in Miami. He threatened to sue when a friend of Richard Nixon, Dana C. Smith, ran up gambling debts of over $4,000 on a little junket with Nixon in 1952. "Rothman was a New York City bookmaker, who made it big in Cuba... Rothman began running guns to Castro...like most U.S. mobsters, figured that Castro would cut the mob in for an even bigger Cuban take, if he got guns and ammunition when he needed them"—Kantor. Ruby turned FBI informant. The Warren Commission overlooked his courier role for Rothman and Trafficante. Connections existed between Lansky's courier Jim Braden and Ruby. Braden was on parole for mail fraud and interstate transport of stolen property when he ended up in Dallas in late 1963, about the same time as Ruby. Braden may have met with David Ferrie, Oswald's acquaintance from his days in the Civil Air Patrol. Ruby also had connections to Sinatra's Reprise record company. Calls to Sinatra confidant Mike Shore coincided with a call to Irwin Weiner, an associate of Giancana, in Chicago. A few months before JFK's assassination, Giancana met with his connections in Dallas at Ruby's Carousel Club to discuss the bookmaking business. After Ruby shot Oswald, Ruby's brother Earl, who knew Shore when they were both children, called him to find an attorney for his brother. Following his arrest, Ruby was kept in a windowless cell for thirty-two months, where some report that he often ranted incoherently. He would soon die of advanced cancer with metastasis all over his body.

10.Six years after Hecht's death, *Scanlan's Monthly*, a short-lived, somewhat radical periodical, published the remains of his writings about Mickey, and included humorous anecdotes of their vacations in which Mickey was always a fish out of water. The rare *Scanlan's* article was twenty pages, including photos. Columnist Leonard Lyons had predicted that the article would reach 25,000 words. Perhaps Hecht never got much more down on paper, or editor Sidney Zion had reduced the article size for publication. Zion had promised that *Scanlan's* would "... carry out an unreasonable editorial policy which would vilify the institutions so dear to the hearts of most investors." He also promised to jumpstart Hecht's literary renaissance.

[11].Harry ran a dress shop in Simi, California, named Cathy-Rose Fashions.

[12].Nixon curried favor with some of the most sullied people in America, and arranged deals that would have impressed the most ingenuous criminal. He slyly rose to power through a symbiotic relationship with mobsters, investment bankers, CEOs, and wealthy families. During the 1950s Meyer Lansky had the blessings of Cuba's Batista, who was the beneficiary of tons of cash. Then Vice-President Nixon embraced the Batista-Lansky gambling connection, and ignored Cuba's socio-economic problems. His lifelong pal Bebe Rebozo had shares in Lansky's Cuban gambling haven, a short flight from Miami. Another Havana partner was Moe Dalitz, someone Nixon had to ignore when making his Washington reports. Nixon was a heavy gambler, and received comps whenever he traveled to Cuba. Lansky wasn't alone; Rebozo associate Santos Trafficante and Johnny Rosselli shared in the largesse offered by upscale gambling in Havana. The Rebozo connection linked Nixon to mobsters all over the country. Nixon's Florida real estate holdings came as

a courtesy of lenders who also did business with Jimmy Hoffa and Meyer Lansky. Watergate hush money suggested funneling from the coffers of gambling czar John Alessio, Howard Hughes, Carlos Marcello, and Tony Provenzano. Conspiracy theorists make the most out of Nixon's bad memory regarding his whereabouts at the time of the JFK assassination; he utilized several versions about how he had learned of JFK's death. He had been in Dallas at a Coca-Cola board meeting just before the shooting. Joan Crawford and Nixon bragged to local reporters how they didn't require Secret Service protection, perhaps embarrassing JFK into reducing his own security plans. Speculators loved to pin on Nixon the reason that JFK did not use a Plexiglas top on his limo. The Giancanas wrote about Nixon's life-long help with government contracts and even bailing Jack Ruby out of a jam. The authors claim that Sam Giancana spoke of the Lyndon Johnson and Nixon complicity in the JFK assassination. "When Nixon died I thought of the Shakespeare quote about the evil that men do living after them, and the good being interred with their bones. With Nixon the reverse was happening: They wanted the good to live on and the evil to be buried"— Anthony Summers. "If there was a candidate for the presidency whom the mob wanted elected, it was Richard Nixon. Since the earliest days of his political career in California, Nixon had seemed to walk hand in hand with the Mafia..."—John Davis. "Santos [Trafficante] viewed Nixon as a realistic, conservative politician who was not a zealot and would not be hard on him and his mob friends. The Mafia had little to fear from Nixon"—Frank Ragano. Many still argue that a vicious Democratic smear campaign tarnished Nixon's legacy, at least with regard to mobsters.

[13].Pat Nixon was not fond of Chotiner or any of her husband's other shady connections. Richard Nixon had an agenda, an early architectural design for power, knew that the mob would always be helpful, and never heeded his wife's warnings. "But when she [Pat Nixon] voiced her disapproval, my father decided Chotiner's hard-line, street-smart political advice was more important to him than his wife's objections. So the subject of Murray became a non-subject"—Julie Nixon Eisenhower.

4.

[1]. In 1970 Marlon Brando-look-alike Marcello had his photo taken by Christopher R. Harris at a Louisiana State Senate Hearing in Baton Rouge. He never paid taxes on his extensive Louisiana businesses, while his mob controlled the entire state. The tight web of politics and organized crime coexisted in a world where jazz and well-prepared gumbo fronted for reality. Authors have linked Marcello to the Martin Luther King assassination.

[2]. Nixon's nefarious backers list compiled by author John Davis included Allen Dorfman, "mob-connected Teamsters financial 'consultant' from Chicago (who was murdered gangland style), Mafia-backed Teamsters vice-president Tony Provenzano, and southern California Mafia figure John Alessio" and Murray Chotiner, a "California mob attorney." Dorfman once told mafia attorney Frank Ragano that payoffs were made directly to President Nixon's aides to reduce Jimmy Hoffa's prison sentence.

3. "I am presently serving a sentence in the federal prison in Alcatraz. At my request, I asked for a meeting with a state law enforcement officer, and on October 9, 1962, Richard R. Rogan met with me in the visitor's room at Alcatraz. I informed Mr. Rogan that I wanted to discuss with him a question concerning the influence of persons engaged in gambling and bookmaking on the early political career of Richard Nixon. I first met Richard Nixon at a luncheon in the Goodfellow's Fisherman's Grotto on South Main Street in 1948. The meeting was arranged by Murray Chotiner, who asked me to meet Mr. Nixon, who was about to start his first campaign as a representative in Congress that year. I was asked by Nixon and Chotiner to raise some money for Nixon's campaign. In either 1948 during Nixon's second race for Congress or 1950 in his campaign for the senate, I was again asked by Murray Chotiner to raise funds for Nixon's campaign. During that time I was running most of the gambling and bookmaking in Los Angeles County. I reserved the Banquet Room in the Hollywood Knickerbocker Hotel on Ivar Street in Hollywood for a dinner meeting to which I invited approximately 250 guests who were working with me in the gambling fraternity. Among those who were present, whose names are well known by the law enforcement officers, were Joe and Fred Sica, Jack Dragna and George Capri. Also present was Hy Goldbaum, who is one of the pit bosses at the Stardust Hotel in Las Vegas, who also served a term of imprisonment at the federal prison at McNeil Island. Capri was one of the owners of the Flamingo Hotel in Las Vegas. Murray Chotiner told me I should have a quota of $25,000 for the campaign. During the course of the evening Nixon spoke for approximately 10

minutes. Chotiner spoke for half an hour. At this meeting my group pledged between $17,000 and $19,000 but this did not meet the quota set by Nixon and Chotiner and the group was informed they would have to stay until the quota was met. In addition to helping Mr. Nixon financially, I made arrangements to rent a headquarters for Nixon in the Pacific Finance Building at Eighth and Olive Streets in Los Angeles, which was the same building occupied by Attorney Sam Rummel. We posted Nixon signs and literature, and I paid for the headquarters for three to four weeks in that building. During the period that I ran the Nixon Headquarters, I contacted most of the gambling fraternity in Los Angeles County to tell them what their share of the contribution to the Nixon campaign would be. I have been asked by several newspaper persons and television employees of NBC during the 1956 presidential campaign to make these facts known, but until now I have refused to do so. In view of the fact that Mr. Nixon is now making speeches in his campaign for governor and stating that organized crime is active in California and that Eastern hoodlums were seeking a foothold in California to organize bookmaking, I have decided that the people of California should know the true facts with Nixon's entry into politics being based upon money raised by me and my associates in the gambling fraternity who started him off with $25,000. There have been no promises made to me of any kind or nature and the above statement has been given by me freely and voluntarily"—Mickey Cohen (Released for Publication in 1968). "What the gamblers got in return is spelled out in the records of the Los Angeles County Court between 1949 and 1952, which show that Nixon's campaign manager, Murray Chotiner, and his brother, acted as attorney in 221 bookmaking and underworld cases. In almost all instances their clients got off with light fines or suspended sentences"—Drew Pearson. In a telephone conversation with the author on October 25, 2006, revisionist Nixon scholar and biographer Irwin Gellman mentioned how Nixonphobic biographers before him had too readily repeated the shady fundraising tales and smear campaign politics. Historian Gellman reported that in his exhaustive new research, including diaries, Nixon does not mention receiving money directly from Mickey Cohen; the connection relies too heavily on folklore.

5.

[1]. Attorney Sidney Korshak used his muscle on Kirk Kerkorian, the major shareholder of MGM, engaged in building the new Vegas hotel of the same name, and asked that he release Al Pacino from his contract to play Michael Corleone. A work stoppage at the hotel's construction site by powerful labor leader Korshak would have been costly to Kerkorian. Legendary producer Irwin Winkler had bought the theatrical rights to Jimmy Breslin's *The Gang That Couldn't Shoot Straight*. Winkler already had Al Pacino slated to play the lead when David Begelman, then managing Pacino, let Winkler know that there was a problem. Frank Rosenfelt, head of MGM, called Winkler personally to describe the Korshak phone call to Kerkorian. Winkler substituted Robert DeNiro in the lead role, which led to many further creative associations: *Raging Bull; New York, New York; Goodfellas; Guilty by Suspicion;* and *Night and the*

City. (Begelman committed suicide in the chic Century Plaza Hotel after an evening with Sandi Bennett, former wife of fabled singer Tony.)

2. The headliners in the early seventies included Sammy Davis, Jr., Elvis, Liberace, Englebert Humperdinck, Rowan and Martin (Ciro's former bartender), Don Rickles (a Mickey favorite), Debbie Reynolds, Johnny Carson, Perry Como, Barbra Streisand, and Andy Williams. Attorney Sidney Korshak negotiated a famous one-million-dollar contract for Reynolds, and represented Barbra Streisand and Dean Martin.

3. Jay Sarno and Nate Jacobson ran Caesars Palace. Sarno later started Circus Circus. Dalitz, Morris Kleinman, and Sam Tucker operated the Desert Inn. Sidney Wyman, Al Gottesman, and Jake Gottlieb ran the Dunes. The Riviera elite were Ben Goffstein, Willie Alderman, and David Berman. Milton Prell started with the Sahara, and later resurrected the Tally-Ho, which became the Aladdin. Allen Glick fronted the Stardust, Fremont, Hacienda, and Marina hotels. "Dandy Phil" Kastel, under the auspices of Meyer Lansky, spearheaded the Tropicana. During the modern era, Arthur Goldberg (Park Place Entertainment), Sheldon Adelson (Sands), Steve Wynn (Mirage, Bellagio, Wynn), and Sol Kerzner (Sun City) would run casino complexes.

4. Mickey, who had no health insurance, paid thousands of dollars in cash before treatment. In addition, he paid $250 per day during his short-lived stays in the facility.

5. La Famiglia owner and ubiquitous Rat Pack host Joe Patti said that Mickey was involved during the application process, but despite later investigations,

authorities could not link Mickey directly with the restaurant.

6.

[1]. Matteo's was Sinatra's favorite restaurant. He knew the owners/brothers Mattie and Mike Jordan (who were on hand every night) from Hoboken. They named the annex next door to Matteo's, Little Taste of Hoboken. Sinatra's booth in the back of the main restaurant was only for him, and maître d's still refer to it to as "Sinatra's booth."

7.

[1]. A plausible, but hardly ironclad case suggests that Nugent did have CIA affiliations. During one trip to Africa, authorities detained *Newsweek* writer Nugent and held him in custody on suspicion of being a CIA agent, who naturally was not welcome. He once wrote a detailed documentary for David Wolper about Stanley and Livingston's travails in Africa. During the Soviet invasion of Czechoslovakia, authorities suspected Wolper of CIA associations. Suspiciously absent in Mickey's book is any reference to the CIA; the index is CIA-blank. Three minor mentions of the FBI exist. FBI files avoid Mickey's relationship to Nixon, the Kennedys, Marilyn Monroe, or Sinatra's Rat Pack.

[2]. Audiences unknowingly watched actors perform high on television and in the movies. Business was booming for the drug traffickers; anyone in the drug business was raking in the dough. Mickey refused to discuss

anything having to do with narcotics, and he always stuck to the same story—no drugs. The syndicate had spent decades organizing the flow of illegal drugs into the United States. After years of development, mostly in Europe, the drug trade became a permanent international enterprise. "The criminals who took part in the transformation of the international traffic in drugs by migrating to the manufacturing end represented a variant of modernity itself—they were relativistic, lurid, and urbane"—Alan A. Block. Mickey lived to see pharmacies dispense thousands of Quaaludes each month to 'lawful' prescription-carrying yuppies, who had received their triplicate narcotic drug forms—with directions to cooperative pharmacists—from "pain centers" organized all over the country, many in chic neighborhoods.

3. Frank Sinatra posed for one the most famous mob photographs of the era. All smiles, he took his place at the Westchester Premier Theater, a popular mob-run location, with Paul Castellano, Carlo Gambino, Richard Fusco, Jimmy Aladena Fratianno, Thomas Marson, Gregory De Palma, and Salvatore Spatola. Despite Hoover's hatred for Sinatra, not a single fact in Sinatra's monstrous FBI file would result in an indictment. The Friars Annual Testimonial Dinner finally got around to honoring him.

4. Rosselli, who married actress June Lang (Valasek) and produced movies, once took a beating by restaurant owner Kurt Niklas in his popular Beverly Hills Bistro Garden, now Spago. Attorney Sidney Korshak told Niklas to stay in a hotel overnight until he could reach Rosselli, who never returned to the restaurant. The Bistro Garden would close when business suffered

after Niklas' son Christopher, who seated patrons, insulted a diner with anti-Semitic remarks.

Epilogue

[1]. Corpulent Herbie liked to hang out in Vegas, which still had its strong connections to Los Angeles. He was a lieutenant for Tony Spilotro, who ran the Hole in the Wall Gang, and had a nice run working for him until 1986, when someone buried Spilotro and his brother Michael alive in an Indiana cornfield after clubbing them unconscious. Nobody seemed to care about Herbie's activities, since he was hardly making a dent in the national syndicate. His regular source of income came from loan sharking and insurance fraud, and he operated out of his own auto repair shop. Robert Panaro from Buffalo conspired with locals Carmen Milano and Stephen Cino to take over Herbie's business. Herbie's last words were "Why me? What did I do?" before he was riddled with bullets in his Las Vegas residence. Authorities made a big deal out of his friendship with famous Las Vegas casino operator Teddy Binion, a popular gun-toting Texan who knew how to cater to the little man. Because of Herbie's "Vegas connections," prosecutors and federal investigators suggested that his downfall at age sixty-three signaled the end of organized crime in Los Angeles.

Made in the USA
Columbia, SC
14 May 2020